CW00889272

SUBSCRIPTIONS TO DREAM CATCHER MAGAZINE

£18.00 UK (Two issues inc. p&p)
£25.00 Europe
£28.00 USA and Canada

Cheques should be made
payable to **Dream Catcher**
and sent to:

Dream Catcher Subscriptions
161 Lowther Street
York, YO31 7LZ
UK

+44 1904 733767

argillott@gmail.com

www.dreamcatchermagazine.co.uk
@literaryartsmag
www.stairwellbooks.co.uk
@stairwellbooks

Dream Catcher Magazine

Dream Catcher No. 50

ISSN: 1466-9455

Published by Stairwell Books ///

ISBN: 978-1-917334-14-3
p10

York UNESCO
City of Media Arts

Contents – Authors

FEATURED ARTIST
ARTIST STATEMENT: JAKE ATTREE

An aspect of contemporary painting that continues to puzzle the casual onlooker is subject matter. Sunrises, galloping horses, sheer mountaintops are all, for a variety of reasons, established and preferred themes for many people. It is the message that carries the kernel of truth, the content that imparts the meaning, rather than relatively slippery notions of medium.

Painters such as York born artist Jake Attree, however, have begged to differ for decades.

With an increasing yearning to harness his view of the world via application and observation rather than simple composition, Jake pushes paint around with the chutzpah of the showman and the acuity of the poet. There's a reverence for the subject matter, to be sure, but it is the rococo of the application which primarily arrests, creating a concrete visual space that is all the richer for its heft. There are scumbled dry marks, succulent slabs, crenulated and fossilised attacks, and leathery, wriggling streaks, all serving not only to petrify the subject, whether it's a street or a building or a row of trees, but also inviting the viewer to physically participate in contemplating its depiction.

There are lyrical similarities with poetry here. Perennial favourite, Seamus Heaney, described a poem as a "setting apart of language – making a 'thing' of it and housing it differently". Jake sees, before the rest of us, the potential of this concrete presence, not only in the things itself, but in the art which skewers it. British poet Ruth Padel would perhaps call it the "the texture of the now", a vitally rich invitation from the artist to not only step into the materiality of the painting, but to dwell in it. Poet Emily Dickinson considered poetry to be as rich as a painting and richer than prose:

> I dwell in Possibility –
> A fairer House than Prose –
> More numerous of Windows –
> Superior – for Doors –

It is this opportunity to explore the painting that perhaps provides the building block of genius in Attree's output. Depicting a street scene with all of its bustle and noise is one thing: to inculcate in the same subject matter a unique inner life, at once familiar and completely new, via the kind of mark making that has ensured painting has remained a vitally relevant medium, is the litmus test of a true artist.

Greg McGee

PAGES OF ARTWORK

In preparing DC 50, it was a delight to chat with Emily Zobel Marshall for the second in our new feature of 'The Editor in Conversation with …': I hope you find it as illuminating as I did, and if you wish to contact me about possible subjects for this series – or anything else relating to the journal – do email me on hannahstone14@hotmail.com. I'd also like to extend a warm welcome and many thanks to Laura Strickland, a poet from the wilds of north Yorkshire, who has joined the editorial team. I've really enjoyed engaging with her in various poetry events and I am sure her insights and take on our submissions will be invaluable. You can read more about her on the Stairwell website.

This November, I write to you from the comfort of my stove-side, looking out into the garden where the last roses are wearing snow bonnets and the blackbirds are enthusiastically mining the final windfall apples of the year. Both snow and apples (and, I guess, blackbirds) are modelling their ephemerality, and 'this too will pass' is a mood I have been trying to capture at a time of global chaos and catastrophe. Of course, due to confirmation bias, our choice of news media, what we see on our 'socials' (be it the burgeoning passage of Bluesky or pigeon post), and the conversations we have (or avoid) reflect our own interests and concerns. I know that whatever I write, both here and in my reviews, is going to be subjective. Equally subjective is the focus of our submissions for any given issue.

In terms of the zeitgeist of DC 50, a mood of nostalgia seems to have overtaken our writers. More recent wars are refracted into memoirs of WW1 and WW2; poets and storytellers share childhood experiences; teenage crushes; farewells to elderly parents; lost lovers, alongside some 'je ne regrets rien' moments; encounters with aliens and selkies, and medics giving unwelcome diagnoses. The poetry books reviewed also visit some important pages of the history book, and it was a special pleasure to commission Nick Allen to review Sarah Wimbush's STRIKE, such an innovative example of Stairwell's publishing.

As editor it falls to me to sequence the successful submissions in whatever way pleases me and I hope you take as much delight as I did in the opening and closing poems, both of which caused my heart to soar; don't we all need a plumber like Geoff, and a poet like Julia to give Smart's poem such a witty new lease of life. And how I lived so long without knowing about 'thicc dads' and 'box mods', I don't know: every day a school day.

Fifty issues is A LOT of Dream Catcher, and I am indebted to Alan/Rose for their piece reflecting on this. I know that I stand on the shoulders of other editors and it is an honour to offer what I can to this manifestation of creative self-expression. All power to their elbows; as publishers they do so much of the heavy lifting.

Hannah Stone

We never thought when we published Issue 25 that we would be doing something similar for Issue 50. There has been some 12 odd years between the two but there are striking similarities. We had just taken on the responsibility for Dream Catcher with Issue 24 and the founder, Paul Sutherland, was still the editor; and we were feeling our feet over the format and some of the publishing logistics. We increased the sticker price to £8 and the subscription price to £15 and refreshed the layout of the front cover.

Change has been slow, as befits a magazine that publishes twice a year. We have managed to more than double the number of subscribers which enabled us to start printing the interior art work in colour. The balance between poetry and prose has changed in favour of a little more prose and there are more reviews. We have been able to maintain the eclectic nature of the content without compromising the quality. For this we salute the editors: John Gilham, Wendy Pratt, Amina Alyal and Hannah Stone.

But back to the similarities. The covers have a remarkably similar palette, though issue 25 is of Australian rocks, the colours of which seem to match the 16 hues of gold (Google! Bite us!) Alan was able to find while designing the cover for Issue 50. Readers may have noticed that the cover price has crept up over the last couple of years: this is more to ensure there is a pittance left over after distributors have taken their not inconsiderable cut; but it has become necessary to increase the subscription price from this year. While the price of paper has increased, the real driver has been the cost of mailing which has consistently been above the amount of inflation for the whole 12 years.

There is a heartfelt thanks to the Dream Catcher readers who supported this year's *Poetry for All*: there is still a shortfall for this year and, we are planning next year's performance. (28th November 2025.) There will be two links on our web site, one for this year and one for next, though any surplus from this year will be rolled over to next year.

Finally, we would like to thank everyone who has served on our editorial board, past and present, for the time and support they offer us, the publisher, and Hannah, the editor.

We now look forward to the Diamond edition.

Alan Gillott, Rose Drew

HS   Emily, thanks so much for engaging with me in this conversation, for our special 50th issue. As I did with Bob Beagrie in our last issue, we'll explore issues to do with your writing and identity as a writer – and I'm sure other topics will surface too. First of all, I know that certain myths and traditions from your cultural heritage often inform and shape your writing; would you like to say something about this? As a poet who has written a lot of poetry about Wales, I'd be interested to hear both about your Welsh and Caribbean threads.

EZM   I grew up in a remote farmhouse called Garth-y-Foel near the village of Croesor in Snowdonia, North Wales. My mother and father moved to Garth-y-Foel in 1980 when I was two years old, after living for a number of years in a commune in Buckinghamshire. They wanted to get away from the pressures of communal living and my father had fallen in love with the house on a visit to Wales during the summer. It was a mile long walk from the tiny village road, inaccessible by car and it stood in the middle of a field of foxgloves like an enchanted cottage.

HS   What was it like being a person of colour in a remote corner of Wales?

EZM   My mother was born in Martinique in the French Caribbean, the daughter of well-known writer Joseph Zobel. When she moved to Garth-y-Foel she used to joke that she was the only Black woman within a 50-mile radius. My mother was very much welcomed in our small village in North Wales as a Black woman – a fellow sufferer of Saxon oppressors, whereas my father, a white Englishman, found it harder to integrate, even though he learnt Welsh. I've written about my mother's connection to the culture as a Caribbean woman in the poem *Mamwlad* in my collection *Bath of Herbs* (Peepal Tree Press, 2023).

HS   From my frequent visits to Wales I've picked up on that sense of some Welsh communities feeling the yoke of English colonialism. Your time in Croesor sounds the perfect start for a poet who is so sensitive to the natural world; was it influential on your nascent creativity?

EZM   In my poetry I often explore the healing power of the natural world. I have faced several traumas in my family, in particular health traumas, and even though I now live in Leeds and no longer amongst the mountains of North Wales, whenever I can I try to get out onto the fells. I also like to immerse myself in the waters of the local river Wharfe and swim there all through the year. Many of my poems are dedicated to this experience of seeking out solace in wild spaces – and exploring how wild spaces echo the longings of wild women who refuse to be bound by the constraints of society.

HS   That's a powerful message for us to hear; were there other poets, especially female ones, whom you read on your journey, who voiced that imagery?

EZM I have been very influenced by Peepal Tree Poets on my poetic journey, in particular British-Caribbean poet Malika Booker. I find her work so rich and searing – she gets straight to the heart of the thing, and her rhythm and form are completely immersive. I always return to the work of African American poet and activist Audre Lorde, who described herself as a 'black, lesbian, mother, warrior, poet'; her poems move from languid to fiery, always surprising and challenging. I read her when I need inspiration. I also love the Scottish poet Nan Shepard, who wrote about her profound connections with the Cairngorm mountains in the 1940s. She used to sleep out on the high plateaus of the Cairngorms, and she writes about the mountains as if they were her lovers, capturing all the minute detail of that magical natural world in ways which sing off the page and transport you there amongst the burns and crags. I read and re-read the imagist poets H.D. and Amy Lowell, who were trying to capture the world in direct, clear and vivid language in the early 20th century, and Anaïs Nin. I am also excited by the nonconformist ways in which these women lived their lives/loves in such patriarchal worlds. My favourite male poets are Kei Miller, Roger Robinson, Seamus Heaney and Danez Smith; like Malika Booker, they cut straight to the heart and use language in exhilarating new ways.

HS   How did these early years in Eryri shape your creative development?

EZM My childhood was one of incredible freedom, of being able to explore the 90 acres of land belonging to the aristocrat from whom we rented our house, and I was lucky enough to have a horse and spend time galloping bareback across fields and ridges, pissing off farmers and swimming in the freezing cold rivers. From a young age we were allowed to roam far from home; my mother had a sheep-dog whistle she would blow at the end of the day to return us for dinner before nightfall.

My childhood was connected to Welsh landscapes and culture in a very profound way. I did my schooling through the medium of Welsh – we were not allowed to speak English in the playground at break time – and our community was committed to keeping the Welsh language alive. I was also immersed in African and Caribbean culture; my mother worked for the BBC World Service writing African and Caribbean music programmes and my brother and I coveted her reggae and West African music records.

HS   My brother, who has moved to North Wales more recently than your parents, has spent many hours learning Welsh and 'passes' for Welsh at times! Of course there is the complication of whether you've learned the right Welsh for your location, but I think it has helped him integrate. Do you still speak Welsh? Has it remained an important thread in your creative life?

EZM I speak Welsh and French. My poetry collection interlaces my Welsh and Caribbean roots, exploring my matrilineal line and the sacrifices the women in my life have made for me, as well as celebrating acts of love between women that often go unnoticed.

My grandfather grew up in colonial Martinique in an impoverished cutting cane village and wrote about his childhood in his semi-autobiographical novel *Black Shack Alley* (1950), now published in the Penguin Classic series, which was later made into the film *Sugar Cane Alley* (1983). It is through the sacrifices of his grandmother that my grandfather was able to attend school – she cut cane so he didn't have to; this too has been a story I've wanted to tell in my poetry. Those sacrifices that my great-great-grandmother made also reverberate down to me – I wouldn't be enjoying this life and its privileges if she hadn't made those decisions.

HS   As well as a being a poet you hold a significant academic role (on which many congratulations by the way!). I know that my own writing often entails research and can spring from facts I have gathered whilst working on less obviously 'creative' writing; does this happen for you? Can you give examples?

EZM Thank you, I'm so pleased to have been made a professor this year! My academic work has centred around my Caribbean heritage as well as being inspired by my father's politics. My father, Peter Marshall, is an anarchist philosopher, so I grew up in a family of writers and thinkers and our evening meals were always dominated by tense debate. My scholarly focus has been on Caribbean carnival as well as an African-rooted folklore, always with an emphasis on how cultural forms can be used as forms of resistance and survival in the face of oppression.

I do also draw from 'facts' discovered in the process of my academic work in my creative writing. My first academic book, *Anansi's Journey: A Story of Jamaican Cultural Resistance* (UWI Press, 2012) was about the trickster spider from Caribbean folklore; having an intimate knowledge of this cunning character means that whenever I try and write about boundary crossing in my poetry, I always return to the figure of Anansi. I can manifest him into my work easily. In my poem 'Anansi Mothers' I call for the power of Anansi to find strength, and I think there is some of his trickster energy at work in me.

Another area of research has been for an activity outside of the university: in the last couple of years, I've been training for my mountain leadership qualification. If I do qualify, I'll be the third woman of colour in the country to be a trained mountain leader – it's not a very diverse scene! As part of my training, I loved learning about the synoptic forecast – how various bands of pressure create weather systems. In my next collection, *Another Wild*, I have two poems linking relationships and emotional states with weather systems entitled Synoptic Forecast I and II. They are quite light and romantic. I also have poems dedicated to commemorating David Oluwale's story and the Postcolonial poetry that I teach in class always has ways of seeping into my writing.

HS   It feels to me like you are very much a poet who lives in and responds to community and I see this manifest in your work for the David Oluwale Memorial Association: could you say something about this?

EZM I've been on the board of the David Oluwale Memorial Association (DOMA) for nearly a decade and I'm now Co-chair of the charity with the current Leeds Lord Mayor Abigail Marshall-Katung. We are a small charity who focus on anti-racism and fighting homelessness and ill mental health. I like to be an academic who is public-facing, looking beyond the ivory tower and connecting with communities outside academia. David Oluwale, as many of you will know, was a Nigerian migrant who came to Leeds as a stowaway and was hounded to his death by two Leeds police officers. He was found drowned in the river Aire in 1969.

At DOMA we use arts as a platform to call for social justice and we always maintain that art is deeply political. We were thrilled to have the new sculpture in Leeds commemorating David's story by Yinka Shonibare, 'Hibiscus Rising', which was commissioned by DOMA and supported by Leeds City Council and Leeds 2023. In the run up to the 2023 sculpture launch, I worked with Peepal Tree Press poet Sai Murray to run a competition of writing and artwork which responded to the Oluwale story. We were inundated with incredible responses (with a winning entry from you, Hannah!) from all around the world. It was really hard to make a final choice, but eventually we managed to collate the very best works into the edited collection *Oluwale Now: An Anthology of Poetry, Prose and Artwork* (Peepal Tree Press, 2023).

It was poets, writers and artists who kept the Oluwale story alive and called for justice in the decades after his death. I believe that art and writing can be used as a tool for empathy, to help us walk in the shoes of others, and this is unique. Through poetry we can access the emotional state of people across time, all over the world. It is a powerful tool in helping us keep faith in our shared humanity.

HS   Absolutely; is DOMA planning any further creative events of this sort?

EZM Yes, we have events planned for the coming year. We had a lovely little festival called 'The Nice Up' which was called a 'mini festival of joy and togetherness' by the Hibiscus Rising sculpture in September, with African and Caribbean music, food, crafts and poetry and we will be making them an annual event, animating the sculpture with a message of unity.

We also have two 'Black Flanuer' walking tours in November, in collaboration with 'The Being Human Festival' and historian Joe Williams, where we explore the Black histories of our city on foot. We have the annual DOMA lecture and a couple of poetry events in the pipeline too. Do visit our website and sign up to our newsletter [https://rememberoluwale.org] to keep abreast of all these goings on!

HS   You've been published recently; what do you look for in a publisher and how did that process work for you?

EZM My poetry collection *Bath of Herbs* was published by Peepal Tree Press in 2023. They are the biggest publishers of Caribbean writing and the press is run by the tireless editor Jeremy Poynting. They operate outside a back-to-back in Burley and it always strikes me as amazing that such an influential press is run out of such a modest location.

I was part of the Peepal Tree readers and writers group *Inscribe* for several years before I published my poetry book and mentored by British-Grenadian author Jacob Ross. In our creative writing classes, Jacob used to say the key to a good story is to put your character up a tree – and burn that tree down. Nobody wants to read about a character with a normal, regular life, what's fascinating is how they deal with adversity.

When my daughter was diagnosed with leukaemia in 2018, I received the news while I was on Komodo island in Indonesia, up a mountain. I had to rush home, hustling myself onto a series of different planes to get back to Leeds to her bedside. I remember thinking: my tree is burning down, how I react matters, my story starts now. My daughter is well now, but my beloved mother died of cancer whilst my daughter was undergoing her treatment. I put a lot of that pain and trauma – and the ways of combating it through connecting with nature – into my first collection.

HS   What are you working on now; do you have any other plans for future work, especially any collaborations?

EZM I found Jeremy to be an excellent editor to work with, extremely meticulous, and I respected his feedback as much as I did Jacob's. It's a real honour to be published by Peepal Tree and I'm working on the second collection, *Another Wild*, with Jeremy at the moment. *Another Wild* is going to be a collection about wild spaces – about woods, rivers and water and wild women who desire to break away into wild spaces away from the constraints of patriarchy. I've been selected as one of the BBC Contains Strong Language poets next year and I try and write at least one poem every week.

HS   That's great news; when will details of the BBC shows be released? I am sure we will want to book onto those events; the last Contains Strong Language was fabulous.

EZM In 2025 it will be taking place in Bradford as part of the UK City of Culture programme from Thursday 18 – Sunday 21 September 2025. I'm really looking forward to it.

HS   Some poets have very fixed ways and times of writing; how does that work for you, in your busy life?

EZM I tend to write while I walk, sometimes using voice notes, as I find the rhythm of my step helps me with the rhythm of verses and the outdoors both energises and calms me; it put me in a meditative, creative mood. If it's a poem about the outdoors, everything I smell, hear and sense goes into the poem. Then I returned home to edit, trying to keep the feeling alive. When I can't find a quiet space to do this, and the kids are hassling me, I sometimes hide in the loo with my phone to polish the poem off!

HS   Emily, thank you so much for taking the time to have this conversation. To close, is there anything you'd like to say about the pieces of yours we will read in this issue?

EZM Thank you Hannah, it's be such a pleasure and it's always an honour to be published in this beautiful journal. The poems I have chosen to share with you here speak to the things I've talked to you about today – my childhood in remote North Wales, my connection to the Caribbean, the trauma of my daughter's illness and my observations of the natural world. They are the themes I return to again and again – and I'm obsessed with writing about water and rivers at the moment, in particular the way the sunlight snakes and scatters across the skin of the river or the crest of a wave. I still haven't found quite the right words to describe its wonder, and I live in hope that I will.

WHY I HATED YOU AT THE BUS SHELTER

The green wellies are offensive and signal everything I want to
leave behind during my evening out, yet you insist on wearing

them, Dad, and keep moaning that you've driven 30 miles,
walked 2, to drop me off at this bus shelter, where all the other

Llanbedr teens meet, condemned as we are to live in lonely hill side
houses or bible-black streets. I long only to be deep in that shelter, hiding

from the piecing lights of the SPAR, feeling Leon's lips pressed tight,
the hot surge of inexperienced tongue, tasting of Hooch and stolen

fags, so all I ask is that you don't get out the car, Dad, in those
wellies, because it's hard enough being mixed with massive

bushy hair and living deep in the sticks with no telly, without you
dropping me off in our crappy rusty Bedford van, sheepdog barking like

mad in the back and standing there in your wellies, for all to see;
the ultimate *Joskin* thing to do.

Can't you see I'm living in the in-between here, Dad, always on the
borderlands, always left out, so can't you let me have this, surprise bus

shelter invite to hang out with the popular kids. But you do get out and stand
there, rooted, wanting a hug; *You're ashamed of me, Emily?*

Just get back in the van and please leave now Dad I hiss, and your eyes fill.
As you turn away your tufty head catches the glow of the streetlamp, a little

bent over in your battered khaki wax jacket, trailing a smell of mud,
imperial leather soap and pencils, you climb into the driver's seat, engine roars,

exhaust fumes, dog barking getting fainter, only the loud voices now of the bus
shelter boys trying to penetrate Welsh village silence and still I stand apart,

flooded by the image of you, in your wellies, while all other longings peel away
like the smoke from their Benson and Hedges

into the sharp winter's night.

Emily Zobel Marshall

NURSE CHARLOTTE
After Roger Robinson

Into our carnival of despair comes
Nurse Charlotte with her smell of Nivea face

cream & wide brown eyes. She is the one
who rushes our girl up to Intensive Care

who seems to know just what to say & do, and so
young too, traveling with us & the hospital bed

in the lift, her gentle talk sitting on the threshold
between urgency & warmth. Her socks are adorned

with little bows, I notice, as she leads us into two chairs
before our knees give way. This resuscitation room is

orange and our girl is a floppy doll, smooth-headed under the
hospital sheet. Nurse Charlotte sits upright and so neatly, with

her feet side-by-side on the freshly-bleached vinyl floor. *She will
pull through*, she tells us, and her long mascaraed lashes flutter
like a wren's wing
like a beating heart
and I know it's going to be ok because I have accepted
Nurse Charlotte's gift of conviction, seeded it deep in

my being and there it takes root, growing as steady as her
two Clarks brogues planted so firmly on the ground.

Emily Zobel Marshall

MARTINIQUE, I HEAR

lullabies in your name, notes singing between syllables,
Island of flowers, mother's birthplace, you roll across my
tongue sweet as the swaying of my grandmother's

hips dancing *la biguine*, but under the sweetness, a whispering
like the slash of cane-cutting cutlasses wielded by ancestors
buried in unmarked graves in your rich red earth and there

I stand, *mulâtresse*, edges of my skirt lifted by warm breezes
next to the bronze of my grandfather, honouring his world of
words, looking across your southern undulations at the plantation

of his childhood, site of rupture and blood, cutting a trail back to
Benin. All around me hummingbirds seek nectar from deep within
the throats of sunshine-tipped Heliconias and pelicans dive for silver fish

on the distant rolls of the ocean and I wonder how your abundance, your
loveliness which nearly hurts the eye, has also seen us in chains, how
you've spread the roots of *oiseau-du-paradis* over our rusted manacles. Are

you beautiful, Martinique, to distract us from the blood dripping down the
pages of our past? Martinique, I hear lullabies in your name,
but I must not sleep.

Emily Zobel Marshall

TOAD

The woodland Spring is urgent
vivid shoots push through leaf mould,
sky-bound
yet in the muddied pond
the coupling toads
hang silent.

When shouting children drag them
far from the water's edge
they return as one;
the toads still clinging – a clod of forest floor
making slow, ungainly headway
home again.

Threats of hunting herons
do not release his slender fingers,
will not break his endless clutch
across her broad flat back.

The golden domes of bloodshot eyes
inscrutable, but this quiet embrace
of stippled prehistoric skin
pulses stronger than
the fear of endings.

Emily Zobel Marshall

For I will consider my plumber Geoff.
For he is the servant of Water and Gravity, which are Laws unto
Themselves.
For at the crack of dawn he is on the alert.
For in his morning orisons he foregoes the sun to kneel in a malodorous
crawl-space.
For this this done by contorting his body under the U-bend with stoic
insouciance.
For his offices make us clean and comfortable.
For he is usually pretty reliable.
For when his big job in Manchester is done and the emergency that's just
come in he will be here.
For from the University of Life he has several degrees.
For he has manoeuvred the washing machine single-handed.
For he finds a mouse there which has met its Maker.
For he makes me feel useful by asking if I kept the instructions.
For he can sometimes work late against the Adversary.
For he appears to subsist on black coffee, strong, no sugar.
For one job in seven isn't quite sorted. For there may be teething
troubles.
For he counteracts the powers of darkness by his phone torch.
For he is also a passable electrician.
For he seizes the Devil by the horns and knows which way is OFF.
For he possesses the right sized wrench.
For he leaves no tools in his van overnight.
For he is of the tribe of Fixer.
For his explanations lose me. For but at least he doesn't patronise.
For if he meets another tradesperson, they understand each other.
For a lot of good plumbers came from the EU. For but we do not go
there.
For every home is incomplete without one.
For he is not the cheapest, mind.
For he is needed by rich and poor alike.
For he owns a horse.
For his dexterity equals that of any needlewoman.
For with more floods and storms there will always be work.
For his wife works in a care home and gets Covid-tested twice a week.
For he is Gas-Safe-registered, and has an account with Screwfix.
For his son Adam is carrying on the business.
For he gets to know the late payers.
For he takes calls at the top of a ladder.
For you have to be fit though, and not overweight.

For a smart meter is a waste of time in his opinion.
For he has used that dishcloth which will have to go in the bin.
For he is off to Marbella on his jollies.
For he slams the door so hard I will need a joiner.

Julia Deakin

It was a leisurely New Year's morning, sipping coffee, reading, watching the sunrise out my sliding glass door. I had no plans for the day; just resting up from the festivities of the previous evening.

I suddenly saw nine large geese strolling lordly down the sidewalk like nine men of Boston, heads snootily high, chests puffed out, a comfortable, unhurried strut.

Intrigued, I walked out onto my deck. Thirty-three geese had gathered on the gentle slope that led from my apartment to the road. Most were pecking at the grass. Others walked down the sidewalk.

From time to time as many as twelve of them wandered out into the street, stopping traffic. The cars honked at them. The geese honked back just as angrily and didn't budge an inch. They didn't fly, and they didn't hurry in their steps. The cars would wait for an opening, then edge their way through gaps in the slowly strolling mob.

The geese were like a street gang. Confident in their numbers, they owned this piece of turf.

I watched entranced. Suddenly, at some silent call, the geese all stopped in place and stretched their necks to their full length. They turned their heads to face the same direction. Like everything else they had done, the movement was slow and deliberate, filled with a quiet dignity.

It was uncanny. Thirty-three unmoving sentries, stone still, facing some unseen point. Because I turned my head the same way and saw nothing that could have attracted their attention. No movement, nothing that could have emitted a sound beyond my range of hearing.

All at once, the geese spread their wings to full length and began to flap. It was the sound of a score of circus tents flapping in a hurricane. The geese rose. The noise was intoxicating, overpowering. I didn't know the mere sound of wings against the wind could be so loud. It touched something primal in me and felt alien. A force entirely beyond my will or control. The geese began to honk, but not in unison. A cacophony of shouted orders, arguments, conversations.

They were still fighting for position in their formation as they disappeared over the buildings across the way.

My mind followed them in their flight for a while, then returned to my solid, land bound existence, unable to join them on their journey.

Mark Pearce

She isn't carrying any luggage. That would have aroused suspicion. But she is carrying herself with grace. She slips her fingers down her right hip, then leg and takes comfort in the fact that her wallet is safely stowed away in her thigh high red boot. Her wallet and passport, still there. All safely pressed against her calf. A testimony to the fact that Amina Saad still exists – even if only on paper.

She has no idea where she is going. She only knows she has to get away. Away from *him*. As far away as possible. As quickly as possible. The coach isn't very busy, only a few people are on board, and it will be leaving soon.

There is suddenly the all too familiar prickling in her neck, the feeling of someone watching her. The disapproving looks are piercing darts. Amina's stomach is churning. He might come looking for her. But she isn't turning around to check if she is right. Instead, she glances at the driver's rear mirror, spotting an elderly lady who clearly frowns at her outfit. She is wearing a hairnet and pink curler rollers. When she meets Amina's look in the mirror, she quickly looks away and starts searching for something in her handbag. She feels her breathing steady and heartbeat slow down. *Calm down. It isn't him*, she thinks, suddenly angry at her own paranoia.

What was she worried about? From up here she'd be able to spot him first. And didn't her wig and new outfit make her almost unrecognisable? Didn't she look like a regular comic con enthusiast on the way to some weekend adventure? She examines her reflection in the side window and finds a stranger looking back at her, defiantly. Her long, blonde wig which she has fashioned into two pigtails, is falling smoothly over the blue and white striped sailor collar, her ebony curls safely hidden underneath. The blue and white blouse with the crimson mini skirt makes her look much younger, like a boarding schoolgirl going on a trip abroad for the first time. While the high boots counteract this impression, maturing her by at least five years, and could easily place her in the red-light district in Amsterdam.

Amina is sitting close to the driver. Right behind him, because this is where she feels safest: high up, shielded. She is gazing outside the windshield like on a screen in a movie theatre. Somehow everything feels less real. She is in the protected realm of an anime where happy endings are mandatory, and the heroine always prevails. It makes her believe there is a happy ending to everyone's life story, even her own life story. As the light outside starts to fade, tinting the sky black, the movie theatre darkens for the screening to begin. Slowly, it reveals a crescent moon – a pale and crisp wafer restoring her with its energy. Suddenly, she feels wide awake. From the darkened window glass, Sailor Moon is smiling back at her encouragingly: *This is going to work. We're going to be okay.*

She had not found Sailor Moon. Sailor Moon had found *her*. She had introduced herself to Amina in the display of a fancy-dress shop next to the market on Portobello Road. The mannequin in the display window had caught her attention. Its graceful fingers seemed to be pointing at something. As Amina came closer, she followed the outstretched finger and started reading the poster about the upcoming Comic Convention in Birmingham. And suddenly everything had become clear, her escape route illuminated by green neon signs.

Before Sailor Moon, going shopping was the only time she had to herself. It was the only time he let her out of his sight, apart from being in the bathroom. If only for a few hours a week, it was still valuable time she gained to plan her escape. Now, when she felt the walls of their tiny one-bedroom apartment coming closer once more, caging her in, she managed to push them away right before being squashed. When the stench of his synthetic sweat crawled into her nostrils, close to making her retch, Sailor Moon shone her comforting pale light on her and life became bearable once more.

She would take a couple of pounds each week, not more. Until after a few months she had enough to buy what she needed: money for a ticket and her costume. She quickly changed in the fitting rooms, and, as the transformation was complete, left her old clothes behind stashed away in a Sainsbury's plastic bag which she threw into the closest bin. Amina Saad was no more. The future belonged to Sailor Moon.

There is the shuffling sound of bags being heaved from the racks and feet being dragged around the coach. *Birmingham Coach Station*, the driver's voice announces. She awakes as if from a deep sleep. Looking around her, she notices that she is not by herself anymore. The old lady with the pink curler rollers has disappeared. A crowd of people in costumes and printed theme T-shirts are now scattered around the coach. They are chatting and laughing with excitement, getting ready to disembark to their comic con adventure.

The visitors pour out of the coach in a colourful wave into the misty grey. And Sailor Moon allows herself to be swept away with them out into the unknown ending of her own story.

Marlene Hetschko

TIED
(the things bosses say – 6)

You ask me for my motive;
I was there for five years
spewing CJ's lies

tell them I'm tied up at the moment – in a long meeting, I've gone on a
site visit, out for the day, I'm busy right now, I may be some time, I'm
tied up completely 'til Friday, take a message, I'll call them back later,
just get rid of them girl

Then in November
already wintery-dark
he summoned me in, told me to *Sit!* (like a dog)

there's been a decision, a cost-cutting exercise, so sorry – we have to Let
You Go, it's beyond my control (he lied), *my hands are tied. It's*
Nineteen eighty-eight for Christ's sake, we have to move on, I shall have
a computer, I shall work on my own. Let's face it a trained chimpanzee
could do that

At 5 the exotic Architect arrived
ready for him in her shining stilettos
her timing just right. CJ said

if The Wife calls – say I'm tied up with a client, I have to work late
we've a deadline to meet – tonight

In my desk drawer – a souvenir knife from Morocco
for slitting the post with perfect precision
Just right.
– I let myself go

I left them tied up
together
trussed up with telephone wire,
scattered with pretty confetti
– torn quotes and orders,
contracts in triplicate, shredded,
post-it notes, paperclips,
cheap instant coffee –

turned off the lights and
ran for the bus

Helen Pinoff

Landscape by Water (The Red Hill)

4th August 1914.

WONDERFUL news! War has been declared! Germany has invaded Belgium and my heart swells with gladness. Greatness lights up the once sombre horizon. Lives filled with sorrow now clamour with joy. This is immense news of the most welcome kind. Sacred Mars shall scour the putrid runnels of Europe. Ecstasy!

4th August, midnight.

Jenny says no good will come of it. Pa says we'll give the Hun a bloody good hiding. I say when history sounds its call, only the craven can fail to respond. I think…

6th August.

Today I saw the soldiers march through the high street. Arbroath never looked finer. Ships will be taking them to the continent. I can only say I'm jealous. How I wish to be gone from here! How I wish to escape the mediocrity. Jenny says that I'm being selfish but I don't care. Tomorrow I enlist and thus – to glory!

7th August.

It's dawn and I haven't slept a wink. Too excited. Too alive. The birds sang their chorus, like a beckoning to arms. It's as if the world wills it; the universe! This road to conflict has, I think, the highest sanction. Man is only truly noble when amidst the gravest of adversities. The recruitment team will be waiting and the shilling I shall take.

8th August.

It's a glorious summer's day here in Arbroath and I have joined the throng. Yes, I took the shilling and report for training next week in Edinburgh. I must say my goodbyes. I will miss Jenny, my love, and Pa. But a greater purpose has been written and it cannot go unheeded. I feel light and alive and the Angus air tastes sweet. Tomorrow starts another chapter. And I shall be tossed upon the ocean of life.

17th August.

I arrived in Edinburgh, a city of whores and usurers. I reported to barracks and, thus, military life begins in earnest! I can't wait. I've never fired a rifle. I've never fixed a bayonet. To kill or be killed – the ancient equation that has faced every true generation down throughout millennia. I shan't venture into the city: vice lies there; sin and suppuration. Yes, to kill or be killed: this shall be my shining new sanctity. Logic dictates that survival is the utmost responsibility of every true Christian man. Logic dictates that I must rend flesh and do violence. Legionnaires assemble! Cannae itself awaits!

18th August.

The training is hard. I don't want to hurt anyone. I don't want to hurt … The world is so beautiful, you know? It's just so beautiful it makes me want to …

20th August.

News is coming in of what the Bosch have done in Belgium. It is not pretty. Frankly, failure to respond to such atrocities would be a dereliction of our historic duty. We must stand up to tyranny. Barbarism has no place in twentieth century Europe. My path is clear, my duty crystal. I will throw my all into training today. To beat the Hun we must be supermen on the field. Progress cannot be denied!

25th August.

News reaches us of a great battle at Mons. The British Expeditionary Force is in retreat. The Bosch fell upon them in great numbers. But I am not disheartened. We are superior in spirit and character if not in mass. The world's asunder and Satan himself stalks the Earth. To be alive at such times! Such glorious, tumultuous and terrifying times! Is it not a great honour? Is nobility not ascribed to us through such tribulation? I do not yearn for any other age but this and am glad to be alive now – at such a time of reckoning. Only the worthy shall survive these times and come from them shining and stronger. Only the worthy deserve this distinction. The test of the age is upon us and from its fiery tempest I shall not flinch or cower. Such is the bounty bequeathed to every Briton.

25th August, midnight.

At times I doubt myself. At times I doubt the whole rancid show …

27th August.

A new day shines upon us. The training is going very well. We are all growing expert in the art of killing. Such times! Bright blessings there are. Honestly, I can't wait to get out there. Achilles himself was never so fortunate. Edinburgh is a cesspit and I miss Arbroath. But the true initiate must give up former splendours and comforts for the crucible of his ceremony. My generation shall write a glorious testament. I do believe that those who come after will judge us jealously and wish that they too could have been here in this time. This time of Thanatos is all that I ever desired. At last, I shall get to prove my quality, the unknown man who had languished in obscurity. Upon our bayonets the heavens shine their benediction!

1st September.

The war to end all wars: that's what they shall call it. It'll be over by Christmas, they say. Well, we shall see; so long as it's not all over before we get over there and get stuck into the Hun. I have cold steel to whet and an appetite for glory. Every other honest soul here feels exactly the same. We were all born to serve a higher purpose: something that lives beyond us in the realm of the nation state. Call it a vocation, if you like; there is nothing finer. Soon the world will get to see the stuff of what we are made, we, the blessed generation. The Great Game is afoot and we abide by the truth of its mighty shadow.

1st September, midnight.

Autumn is here … Sometimes I think the whole world is going insane. Sometimes I wake up in the night and my thoughts run amok like shadows on my repose. Sometimes I wonder; and yet I truly wonder …

14th September.

News reaches us of a great victory! The Hun has been stopped at the Marne and is in retreat. My prayers go out to all the souls involved in this struggle. Stout hearts we must have. Stout hearts and firm convictions. The price of liberty is often the blood of our finest. This is tragic, yet true and also noble. To take my place among them: such is the stuff of my wanting.

22nd June, 1915.

I've written nothing for months for the life of a soldier is, in truth, very dreary. But tomorrow we sail to Southampton and thence to France. So, the hour is upon us. Maybe Blighty isn't so bad. Maybe I could make a life here, in Edinburgh. I wonder if Jenny would like it here? I wonder if Pa would? Sometimes I think a great sickness infects us all and yet ... the sheer, heart-breaking beauty of being alive; it makes me want to, oh, I don't know, gather the horizon or sing a benediction! Sometimes I wish ...

22nd June, midnight.

You know, life is just this wondrous, burning, glowing thing. Isn't it? And we are but ...

23rd June.

We arrived in Southampton this morning and all the volunteers are ready. To do their duty. To do their best. To do their worst. The horizon is aglow and replete with possibilities. So, why do I get the feeling that we are all about to be sorely tested? It can only be the prospect of combat! Combat is the ultimate test for every honest fellow. And I, for one, am honoured that it has fallen to me to be tried in this way. I know these men of the 5th battalion Black Watch and can say that I am proud to serve with them. We will do Angus proud. We serve the nation; we are in the throes of grace!

23rd June, midnight.

All I ever wanted was the world ... You know, it sickens me, the richness of it: all of it, I mean, the whole thing, everything: life. It sickens me and makes me want to ... and yet I cling to it and know it will pass, like the wind on the meadow. All of it will pass and vanish into darkness. And that annuls my soul like fire annuls the night. In truth, I need this war like the desert needs rain. So, rain on me, O heavens above, till I drown, till I drown and yet am everlasting ...

25th June.

Viewed from this perspective, Europe seems a wasteland. I'm sick of being a soldier and not fighting. But a new reality heaves into view for all of us and, particularly, a new chapter is to be written in the life of Gordon Sutherland. I must write to Jenny soon. She seems very precious to me now, her and Pa both. A great tribulation has been placed before me and I can only pray that I will be enough of a man to face it. I fear running away. I fear not being up to this trial. I fear letting my family and my countrymen down. And, in Jesus' name, I fear dying more than anything. To end this life on the battlefields of France ... such an end would almost be obscene in its banality. Christ, to be killed out here before I've even truly lived. It would almost be a mockery. Yes, I fear deeply. That is, I am deeply afraid ...

30th July.

I get the sense of something terrible transpiring before our very eyes. Something new is promised here: something new and wholly evil. I fear there will be no victory by Christmas. I fear a long and bloody reality exists before us. Who will prove to be the better men, us or the Hun? I don't know. But I can guarantee this: the light of civilisation has been snuffed out in Europe. Sometimes I think I've made a terrible, terrible mistake.

20th September.

I wrote to Jenny and we finally got our orders. We're to move up to the front tomorrow. Thus, I will know the ultimate trial a man can face: deadly combat. I'm afraid, in truth. I'm afraid and feel ever so alone. Even amid all this bustle; even surrounded by my comrades and fellows; even in the drab ranks of this glad army. I don't think I've ever felt so alone. I can't tell Jenny. I can't tell her the truth. I must put up a spirited front for her sake. Nothing was ever achieved by wailing and rending and gnashing one's teeth. These are brutal times. But I am not a brutal man. And part of me is glad to face my fate. To fall on the field would be … would be … well, now. What will be I cannot change. I must be honest with myself and cling to the verities of life that are left me. Who would be a soldier in times such as these? I would. Of course. I must never forget.

2nd October, midnight.

I'm sorry, Jenny. I'm sorry. I'm sorry, sorry, sorry …

4th October.

The front is the stuff of my very nightmares! I came here to face the Hun but I find I'm really facing myself. I find I'm facing the void of my fears and discovering that I'm not equal to this. My God! What if it's all meaningless? What if, at base, it all amounts to nothing? I can't face the enemy knowing this truth. I just can't. I feel my whole life has been a lie. I must …

8th October. Extract from the diary of Captain James Wilkinson, 5th battalion, Black Watch.

A sad business. Today we had to shoot Gordon Sutherland, a private in my company, for desertion and cowardice in the face of the enemy. A sad business. Next of kin will be informed.

Rory MacCallum

A PHOTOGRAPH OF UNCLE ERIC

Because the village homestead was too small
his father's narrow life did not agree –
poacher turned keeper at Squire's beck and call –
he flew the coop and joined up to be free.
Testing motorcycles, his new calling,
spinning through country lane and rutted track,
half man and half machine, all-enthralling,
he raced the time-trial devil at his back.
Drinking the air as golden fields flashed by,
speed was the only reason to survive;
in his new khaki army life he'd *fly*
and every moment know he was alive!
And on the back it says in faded ink:
'Killed forty-one or forty-five, I think.'

Linda Dawe

*(Great Uncle Eric died in a crash testing army motorcycles long before I
was born. I always wondered if it was on that same stretch of road from
Bovington Camp military base where T.E. Lawrence met his fatal
accident.)*

rowan leaves and berries of the mountain *ash, larch*
oak, birch

baronial retreat for a Manchester brewer
at the end of a railway line
tall round chimneys *small children, boys and girls*
captured in black-and-white
sit down, write

local slate and sandstone
that corridor, the passage *times table, two times two and*
1943, school uniforms, a coat

of arms repeated in panelling
and plaster friezes   blue birds woven
through tulips, shuddering in the breeze *breathe in and breathe out*

designed to catch the sun *South   east   left   right*

a village of rooms *a school*
Grade I listed building
the white drawing room   shimmering
light reflected off the lake *the deck   the bridge*
white triangles

of a ship, keeping all of them safe:
the family   their servants *those pupils   their teachers*

the small ghosts of the dead

Fokkina McDonnell

(During the Second World War, Blackwell was used as a school.)

My Mother Stayed Home
(after Caroline Gilfillan – 'Hail Children of the Revolution')

My mother stayed home when my father went to war.
Her war was a different challenge.
Bringing up seven children
And then me for the last part.
Looking back, I see such hardship,
Despair, fear.
But reading her letters, and
Years later talking to her, I saw
Optimism and yes, hope.
She just got on with things.
Reared rabbits for food
Grew vegetables in the garden.
Cooked, cleaned, washed, fed.
Wrote news of home to my father.
Loved him from afar.
Did dangerous journeys in weird vehicles,
To visit when he touched an English port.
She enjoyed life despite war.
Saw her children grow.
Protected them from sorrow.
Made their lives mean something.
My mother was part of an army.
An army that never marched on Remembrance Sunday.
But we knew, didn't we?
We knew their fight, their victory.

Carole Thirlaway

WAR WIDOW – 1948/49

She went from green and yellow
summer fields, Devon hedgerows
of cream cow-parsley lace

into the dark Atlantic waters.
The Queen Mary carried
her with her war baby

to America, to a new life
but the charcoal cities, noise
were like hands around her throat,

so she gathered her small son
and her suitcases and sailed
home, again in steerage;

a rough passage, steely skies,
a choppy crossing, into the fold
of family, bleat of new lambs.

Denise Bennett

Uncivil War

Beware the man who knows just what he wants
and takes it while you wait for him to ask.
Too smart for that – he knows you might say no.
The deed, once done, is done. It can't go back
– the tree cut down, the habitat destroyed,
and he will shrug, at best – your problem, mate.
And so it is, although you talk like you're
a steward of the earth, concerned and baffled
by indifference. Perhaps that's what
annoys him most – that you believe your view
is worthier than his. There is, of course,
no absolute, no yardstick, shared belief
to arbitrate; there's only puzzlement
and hate, mistrust of enemies next door.

Stuart Handysides

They've come for the tree. Two of them in a truck with a mushroom
logo on its side, earbuds sprouting from their beanie hats.
Mushrooms flaring on corporate green sweatshirts.

Grabbing at its bare trunk they yank it clear from its hardcore bed.
Chuck it in the back on a pile of pruned spring finery
where it holds out its white bones.

The truck drives over that depression filled with cigarette butts
cut into an apartment block's shadow. Stuck there to prettify,
the tree never learns its name.

Fungi filaments busy with gossip and provisions buzz right past –
a mycelium could punch its way through the planet's core
to stitch living things together.

Parked in its place is a new tree – two triangles outlined in white,
balanced topiary-neat on a green bicycle wheel guard,
stamped under the saddle *forest* and *GPS tracked*,
pedals planted in skinny weeds that ask for nothing.

Isabel Greenslade

THE HIRELING
(After William Holman Hunt)

Near the quiet river
where my sister and I roamed
across the meadows near our home
an artist came –

two artists who spoke the same
and laboured in the fields,

one a slight chap in his prime,
the other a bearded man burned brown
who met us at the stile
to beg he may portray my face
and form to grace his painting.

He proposed to pay for my employ,
said I should enjoy a spell in London
for him to execute his task,
promised it would not be onerous.

My brother gave permission
and mother was satisfied.
I was nineteen but my betrothed
Robert took me like a child
up to Chelsea to pose.

Then I lodged there for a while –
perhaps I could have stayed.

My hair was gold as ripe corn then,
my cheeks as red as apples
when I played the Shepherd's maid.

Andria Cooke

A DIAMOND CUTTER – WIJNBERG SA 1932

The diamond splits along lines of weakness,
light bounces off the inside walls
and white exits into rainbow hues.
He saws and shaves.
His hands heal over time.

The cutters relax on the veranda,
lie back in wicker chairs.
A black maid serves
men in white shirts.

Scarred fingers
twist round bowls
of smoking pipes.
My grandfather observes.

His eyes follow hands
flick paper rands into
the elusive flames
of matches
to light tobacco.
The notes quiver and curl,
yellow, blue, green.

Loud voices tell
tall stories and stray,
compete, conflict.

My grandfather's silence
cuts through
and shaves their voices.
He hears the smash of glass.
The maid licks red off her black hand.

Rosemary Mitchell-Schuitevoerder

FANTASY WOMEN
(For Lena Headey)

We begin like Venus:
soft curves and golden hair.
Sometimes we're witches.
Often we're fucking someone
who – spoiler – is not our husband.
We bury betrayals and setbacks
with our murdered children
in deep, haunted vaults.
Our words are a finger-snap,
we are infinitely meme-able
especially when the smallfolk
accost us in the street,
strip us, stone us, call us *whores*.
Oh, writers, we are bored of it.
So we'll keep on refusing to die,
bare-breasted, shameless.
We will not repent. We bask
in wild green fire,
we tumble men like cities.

Lucy Heuschen

FANTASY GARDEN CENTRE

I'd feel a bit like Elton John when we got there.
The way I once saw him dash around HMV in a documentary,
raking up handfuls of CDs from the display racks
and dropping them in a shopping trolley
to a soundtrack of Saturday Night's Alright.
While Bruce slipped upstairs to the Paradise Lost Café
to make his phone calls over an Americano and a croissant,
I was left alone to help myself. Buttercup potentillas,
ceanothus, dahlias, marguerites – it all went in.
Bee friendly plants like salvia, scabiosa, Hidcote lavender
and marjoram were always favoured. And how could I resist
a Dreaming Swan anemone or a Guinevere delphinium
for the already crowded crescent bed near hole 13?
Six for ten alpines and reduced annuals
were a cagey nod to a thriftiness I did not feel.
I was poorly paid and this was as close to a bonus as I got.
Later, once I'd found a home for it all
on the adventure golf course, customers became my enemy
with their careless feet and scything clubs,
but all that was far from my mind as I wandered
those alphabetically ordered, scented aisles.
I like flowers, I might have said in my defence if ever
he questioned my extravagance on his return,
although to his credit he never did. Still, I would avert my eyes
when he paused after the checkout to examine
the tapeworm of the receipt, his forehead scored
with that ex-banker's forgery-seeking frown as I pushed
my humming ecosystem towards the freedom
of the sliding doors. We'd load the car up together,
filling the generous boot and invading the papered backseat.
One of the more delicate plants usually ending up on my lap
in the passenger seat – a hollyhock or a lupin perhaps,
laden with buds – as secure as the memory
of sitting on my mother's lap without a seatbelt.

Mark Czanik

At Four, We Are Teaching Her About Maps

When she startled us by reading – the backs
of buses, directions in recipes, junk mail
flung on the kitchen table – we knew we had
someone amazing on our hands. (Well, we
already knew that, but this was a different kind
of amazement.) So, you have printed out
a map of our neighbourhood and she is happy
circling coffee shops and schools and libraries
and of course her parent's bakery. And then
you zoom, and there is all of Germantown, then
Philadelphia, Pennsylvania, the Atlantic coastline,
the Appalachians, the Mississippi and yes
she has the view we might have from the moon.
The moon she has questioned as it follows
our movements in the car. From grandmother's
house to her parents, from pre-school to the stars.

Kelley Jean White

ECHOCARDIOGRAM

Slosh slosh, fluid in a flask,
flutter in a cage, crackle of ice

a bar dimly lit, unpeopled
and you made to wait, watch

on and on, on loop
and the barman in black

who stares past you, beyond the stars,
the black waste, shakes shakes,

stares past you as the bore
ever leaning at the bar.

Nigel Prentice

I'd promised to WhatsApp the photo of Alison and me at Bora Bora and so I did and it's all smiles a beach a big white wheel and as I sent it I smelled the salty tang and I didn't have to wait and here is the message *not such a nice photo* and she's right and I fail to count the black dots on the MRI scan and the neurologist had said popcorn effect and I must reply and I can't think of a Dutch word and no emojis no crosses and did she say raspberries and maybe I'll look that up later and here is the big black one so I just type *interdaad* and press the arrow.

Fokkina McDonnell

SPRING MORNING IN THE SURGERY

My hand palpates an abdomen,
but though I meet my patient's eyes
to reassure and look for pain
my own are drawn across the way
where, up a tree, a harnessed man
swings out and sounds his chainsaw on a branch
that duly falls, scooped up by mates below.

His life appealing on a day like this:
outdoors, with exercise, and circumscribed
– come in, cut down, clear up, ship out, day done
– so different from my settled place of work
I think, and as I watch, my fingers find
what I had hoped would not be there.

My patient's eyes betray no fear for now.
I think of plans abandoned, hopes deferred
and places he would never choose to go.

I have to broach it straight away
he can't go home believing all is well.
He needs some tests, he has to be referred.
He won't sleep well tonight (and nor may I
– at least I'll know I've done my job).

I may have saved his life (put off his death)
but he will know mortality exists
for him – that health will be provisional,
time-limited, dependent on review,
successions of reprieves with any luck,
no freedom from a niggling doubt.

He may not want to see me after this
– he was ok until he came to me,
I'll be the one who gave him his disease.

Stuart Handysides

BEAUTY IN THE EYE OF THE BEHOLDER

He stares at my sun-damaged face,
not quite looking into my eyes
but at my right medial canthal area –
checking the full thickness skin graft
that followed removal of a rodent ulcer.
The fibrous papule on my right nasal tip
gets some attention too.

As if that's not enough for him
he asks, hopefully, if I have
any other lesions he should know about.
I mention the blemish on my outer forearm.
He takes my hand, turns it, scopes closely
and, without looking up, sighs, 'that,
is a beautiful blue mole.'

Ann Gibson

UNFIT BIT

I shall be unhealthier this year.
I shall not go swimming any more.

I shall not clockwatch, feel hot as the hour approaches,
nor sigh and tell myself it must be done.

I shall not curse the sticking cupboard door.
The plastic bags will lie inert, the earplugs twinned.

I shall not drive the six miles thinking *this is silly*,
not creep from cubicle to cubicle to find a dry floor,

not eye men's paunches or pouches,
wonder how their hair has sunk below the neck,

or miss the naiad I apostrophised as FUCK ME,
whose name I don't know, whose tattoo I do.

Julia Deakin

Not CREATURE OF THE SEA

Under the pulling moon
You drop your handbag, your clothes
On rocks blackened with lichen.
Leave your shoes,

To totter, tender-soled
Towards dark water
Seeing the seal
Until her bulk is across your path,

Her mottled head turning
To pin your startled gaze with
Teary eyes.
Putting pictures in your mind.

She shows you an oil-smothered bay.
A rocky coast where men wield bloody clubs, and
Far from land, her mate chokes on
Prawn à la plastique.

Nets scraping the seabed bare.
No fish where there should be fish,
Too many penned where they weren't before,
Sickly and frantic –

Foul water.
She would be human.
She would change sides.
She is weary of losing.

You show her cities and roads and plains of concrete.
Grimy skies
And burnt forests.
You show her deserts.

You try to convey the mass of humanity:
Its needs, its greeds
Blow car fumes across the moonlit beach
She will not be dissuaded.

You show her your hobbled heart
You show her your sadness

Gather images of loneliness and yearning
Thrust forward elusive concepts

But she is of ocean, of being and doing.
Her skin is splitting, peeling away to
A woman cocooned, young and sleek with
Choppy grey eyes.

The selkie folds her pelt with clumsy fingers
Grunts as she hands it over.
Can you? Should you?
The skin's still warm as you wrap it round your body.

Down at the shore, a seal shuffles through the wash of waves.
In water, deep and cool, she
Twists,
Rolls, and dives.

Jan Stacey

Dragonflies as blue as veins born
into this perfect timeframe, this one day;
the loch revealing itself through a stand
of rusting bracken, trees. And now
the shock of cold, waves lulling me like love
to my longed-for selkie form.

Above, a Kite, the harbinger of island news,
delivering cries across the loch to fields
and sea. Its fork and claws much more
than bird – more dinosaur. This day
could be any time at all. This one true
day, lost to water, dragons, sky.

And as I swim, my thoughts settle on my Dad,
who has never learned the art of swimming.
He finds his own perfection sitting at the park
on Mum's memorial bench watching the lighthouse
and far-off ships; no need to reach them.
I turn, cut the loch in two, head to pebbled shore.

Lynn Valentine

Baile Hill, Morning

AT PEACE

(After Edip Cansever's 'The Table', translated from Turkish by Julia Clare Tillinghurst and Richard Tillinghurst)

A woman full of purpose puts the old front door key
onto the slate kitchen worktop. She places
her blue leather handbag there and her car keys.
She puts the picture of what the place was like before
down too. The smell of farm, the chill
of the thick walls, the blackbird singing outside. Dust
on her lips. She puts her renovation plans there,
her dreams for the future, her whole life.
Two plus two equals four and it is complete.
Dad saying to Mam, 'A grand day for a spin.'
The woman sees she has finished most
of what she had to do. She doesn't need to chase
dragons anymore, nor bear the weight
of all her ancestors' lives on her narrow shoulders.

Janet Laugharne

WHEN PAST IS PRESENT

I enter without
my keys my card my phone
only me

I take off my coat my jacket my boots
I spread my legs, stretch my arms
I feel

the zero-policy search down my sides
I listen

I expect to hear
please proceed to gate …
too much noise
trays bump and roll
bag scanners push and spew
limbs with tattooed dragon heads
trapped in tight clothes
search for shoes
cold feet shuffle
I watch

jaws
clenched in featureless faces
follow each other down
never-ending corridors
posters on walls shout
silent warnings
keys clink on belts
worn round waists
to stay entry

heavy doors slide
and we trickle through to
past events that never pass

Rosemary Mitchell-Schuitevoerder

Her yellow coat, the best sight in the world. Her hands, the palms of her hands, seamed and tender. Their touch.

It is the winter of waiting: a cold of icicles. The insides of my knees are chapped blue and red. It's the winter she doesn't meet me from school and I have tuppence for the bus. I get off a stop early and spend the saved halfpenny on salad days and black jacks. The black jacks leave your teeth sticky with liquorice but last all the way up the hill to the house.

It's the winter I panic if she isn't home. I look for clues; smoke from the chimney, her bike at the gate. Sometimes she hasn't lit the fire in the back room, or it's dropped low and she sits at the piano with her coat still on, ready to play. If she's not there, I am not.

Her room is warm, preternaturally. As if we are bringing something on. Her room is disturbing, where I cannot go. The yellow pudding basin frightens me. In the morning it's finished. The house full of release like a rush of fluid, a ripple of calls, the sound fall of doors opening and shutting. Something, or somebody, is crying.

Outside it's snow-dark. I'm allowed upstairs and she's in bed wearing a soft jacket. The lamps are all on. Father is playful. The red stick of baby wails piteously. Another boy they say and secretly I'm pleased. She re-buttons my cardigan done up wrong – puts my hair slide back in, the top of my head reaching for her touch like a cat.

The kitchen is loud and upside down, full of baby bottles and National Dried Milk tins. The baby screams and has displaced us all. In the hall stands the covered airer. It's like a dimly lit tabernacle and I line its wooden slats with white washing, closeting myself, letting the fingers of warm air reach under my gymslip, attentive to my bare knees and thighs. The steamy heat seals my eyelids – and as if I sleep embraced from underneath, distorting its yellow rectangular shape, my cheek pressed against the rough sharp smelling cloth.

Her going upstairs lets in some loud white water where it froths and chafes all afternoon while she lies sleeping. How I long to go there too, drawn like a bee to some waxy honeyed cell. Her room is a haven above the noisy vacancy below, the little ones grizzly, runny nosed, father shouting, the afternoon raw. Later, I am tasked with taking her a cup of tea and the room is drowsy and warm. She sips her tea like a scarcely wakened forest creature at a night pool. I watch my face round and serious reflected three times in her looking glass, the shouts downstairs slipping away as she pats my bare knee.

Sometimes I creep into her room, slipping between the dressing table mirror and the window – the sun condensing yellow and dusty, a secret sleepy place for me to bask, dream, watching the silver backed brushes gleam, the room giving off grown-up smells. Father's Brylcreem sourish from his pillow, her brownish pink face powder spilled from its gilt box, sherbetty – her smell lighter, a blind smell, recognisable like my own. And perhaps we share a leavening which removes us from the clamour of the house, for she comes to sit here, abstracted, letting the mirror give back her face, pausing, as if notes sweetly chisel her private silence. She sees me, bunched and owlish, tells me to go, sending me away, not crossly, not minding me there.

The opening of the veranda is the beginning of summer. She makes it a heraldic occasion. All winter it is shut, a dump for mud-caked boots and bikes; the summer things – garden forks, deck chairs, bucket and spades, inert and clammy. I like its glass roof which traps the sky and insects and how the glass makes days longer. The holiday feel of the doors being open, morning coming in yellow and buzzing. It's best in the halfway season when you can watch the rain fall in big splashes, smell wet mud from the balding lawn.

She drags the kitchen table outside for tea. Bread and jam and cake, our arms all goose pimples. On long light evenings, her dreaming face at the piano, she plays – each note adrift in the green garden. I cultivate my tadpoles in their brimming jars, conceal them under the blackcurrant bush, its small navy berries hard and tight. My little brother chants on his potty upstairs, his urgent rhythmic song spilling through the open window and a gentle chock carries from the bowling green. The front door slams; father's dinner steams under a plate. We think summer will never end and the puppy chews our ankles as we race in and out in a silly game.

There was always a piano in our house. White keys like milk, mild and smooth, some yellowed a little at the rim, as if soured. The black keys stuck up as you ran your hands over the surface, snagging. The piano's white notes dropped through the air on summer evenings; but there were the black notes too – fast and hectic, on and on. Sometimes I'd sit in the room with the silent closed piano and read, filling my head with wild swans, mermaids; the story of Death who snatched the baby, the mother who followed, followed. Then I wished the piano wasn't shut, eased the lid to see the cool milky keys again.

The way she left, I forget. Wind going through the house. Hush.

Denise McSheehy

THE
TERRACES

Is this really the house?
Number Eighteen, it says on the door.
Has the house shrunk in the rain, like wool?
Or have I grown too big,
Like Alice, drinking and eating
Till my head won't fit through the door?
I knew change had come
When I entered the street,
Because all the cobbles had gone.

But yes, this is the house,
It has not moved
In forty years; it stands,
Common sense tells me, unchanged.
Inside, it has a child
Hidden away, but blissfully so.
A brother, a mother and father
Still eat together at Sunday lunch,
With the wireless tuned to Radio Two,
Playing songs from before I was born.
Our cat sits on the windowsill,
Waiting to be let in.
Betsy the car sits out front,
A big black tank of a car.
I wonder if the stairs still creak,
If the cellar stinks of damp,
If the woodchip paper covers the walls.

How I want to go in,
But the past is locked inside.
The door will not let me pass.
It is a new door,
White, when ours was green.
It closes my wondering down.
This is just a house now.
Someone else's home.

Howard Benn

HORI-HORI

They have flown to the underworld now
the swallows, with their knowledge of how we live
when no-one else is watching. The children, too,
are grown and gone. After a night of gales

you zig-zag across the garden under the trees
retrieving fallen branches. One by one
you post them into the thicket of the dead-hedge
then kneel to weed ground you turned

to make a bed for grasses.
Her last day, you held hands with your mother
and talked, and sat in silence,
wholly attentive, wholly given over

to the needs of that separation.
There is dirt under your nails. If I ask,
will you tell me here and now is the only happiness?
Once more you set to, working the hori-hori,

whose name is the rasp of a blade in and out of the earth.

Patrick Yarker

MOTHERING SUNDAY EVE
(9ᵗʰ March 2024, with reference to Hallelujah by Leonard Cohen)

Sifting through a sheaf of old photos
I find her picture –
always a glamour girl
even at ninety something;
her hair swept into a neat French pleat,
slick of 'Hot Coral' on her lips.
We'd tied a tea towel around her neck
at lunch that day, to keep her dress clean
but it looks every inch
like a Jacquard silk square.

She was a song of praise,
a green linnet poised on a feeder.
I can still hear her holding a hymn tune
in her strong contralto voice
or humming a David Whitfield song,
Answer me Lord above …
as she dusted the stairs,
her lusty *Abide with me* at funerals.

That night I dreamt of her last days,
resting in bed, her fingers
twisting her soft loose hair
we'd tied with a blue ribbon.
Then I saw a cobalt sky,
it was twilight;
I was looking down over a beautiful bay
and someone was singing
hallelujah, hallelujah …

Denise Bennett

WHEN I VISIT

She might not remember my name, nor my face
especially when she wakes, sleep-spun, mumbling
for her mum and how she best be getting home.

She'll often look up at the sound of my voice
only to peer past my shoulder, frown,
then turn to an empty chair with a sigh.

Sometimes she'll return my smile to be polite,
then promptly stand to leave the room
as I sit down. *I won't disturb you,* she'll say.

One day she even screamed as I reached out
to squeeze her hand. *How dare you,* she said.
Touching me like that. Who do you think you are?

Yet now and then she knows; three words
leap from her mouth and hook into my chest,
fingers spread across my nose and cheeks to check

I'm real. *I love you,* she'll say, pulling me close
to press her forehead gently against mine;
as if she could fix me there in her mind.

Mims Sully

ADIEU

It was a private farewell.
I opened my window, let you out
with a mayfly batting against glass.

It led you away out over the lawn
as the unsettled trees tried to
sweep the sky clean of cloud cover

as if clearing a way
to the horizon, jagged peaks
stepping stones to the stars.

I had, of course, hoped for
a shadow hesitating, but saw
only emptiness in empty air.

Touched your necklace,
one I wore every day;

found it warm with my
body heat, no longer cold with
your absence of it.

And I was able to say: I kept you
too long. Felt like love, seemed like
life support, yours and mine.

In reply I heard briefly a tired sound
and though I strained my ears
I could not source it.

Stephanie Conybeare

WATERPROOF

This morning, finally, I got round to it –
wiping down her bright blue nylon walking gear:
waterproof cagoule and chest-high trousers
whose striding *swish swish swish*,
mistrusting sunshine, signalled Mum's approach –
the brisk and stoic pessimist.

Scrubbing at muck from that final walk,
I wonder: had she suspicions it would be her last
as she gathered breath against some mossy wall;
hesitant at stile, sure of the narrow gate?
She's farside of those now – all trespasses forgiven.
No need for waterproofing. Home and dry.

Folded clean for Charity, all trace of track,
permissive footpath, pilgrimage erased,
waiting for some new all-weather walker
in search of the impermeable. But listen
still; here's the rub: *swish swish swish;*
this whispered friction, such dry determination.
At Dad's death, too, her eyes did not get wet.

Susan Wallace

THUNDERSTORM

The air is heavy tonight.
I wish it would thunder.
A proper storm
like those of my childhood,
where thunder rumbled round and round,
sharp flashes of lightning
pierced the blackening sky.
The sort of storm you could see coming.
My mother would say "It's black over Bill's mother's."
The sort of storm that afterwards the air
was fresh, newborn, giving relief.
A proper storm which brought the family
together, united by mother's fear.
A storm to bring us down from our beds,
to listen to stories of storm damage,
myths of the dangers and power of lightning,
listen to stories of our parents' childhood,
ghost stories more terrifying than storms.

Tonight I wish it would thunder.

Mary Warner

HAIRCUT

Pre-hippy, and tiffs over hair,
And briefly, sadly, after,
He'd take me to the barber
In Church Road, Acton –
Crisp on top and hard-waved,
Like the young Osgood –

And I'd learn again the balm of tiny relationships,
The way he'd have a quick joke and jaw
With the doormen at recording studios,
Carrying fiddles in his beige case
Like a hood in the field.

I went a couple of times later, without him,
Crew cutting the grief,
The piles of hair on the floor,
Weightless as a soul,
Before it began to wear thin.

Peter Datyner

TOGETHER

In the clear cold air and the black of the night
I pause to look at the shimmering sky,
a vast array of dark and bright,
a keening wind, an awesome sight,
the planet turns, the stars go by.

I sense my father by my side,
together we gaze on the paradigm,
father and son at a great divide
for he is gone but the heavens abide,
and I am here looking back in time.

Waymarks taught by father to son
– Cassiopeia, Orion, the Plough –
he stands and points to hither and yon,
telling the names that will ever go on,
and I remember quietly now.

Alone in the dark, at the end of the day
I pause to look at the black of the sky,
the stars are spread in a vast array,
a keening wind sweeps all away,
we stand together, he and I;
                              he and I.

Philip Dunkerley

LOST IN THE
CROWD

as you grow older
my father said
or would have said
if he had not lost the power of speech

unable to swallow
he was fed through tubes
that by-passed the usual routes
liquid nutrients sped
like a presidential convoy
along roads closed to ordinary traffic

as you grow older
he would have said
things that are hidden from you
in your younger years
come out of the shadows
into the half light

the words were unspoken
but I could read them in his eyes
or would have done
if they had not been closed

now it's your turn
one of my children said
I could not tell which
having lost the power of moving my head

which one of you is speaking?

whether I spoke loudly enough to be heard
or for that matter spoke at all
I could not tell
there was no way of telling which faculty had failed
the faculty of speech
or the faculty of hearing

the problem of identifying the faulty part
like the problem of identifying the faulty bulb
in the fairy lights we used to hang
on our Christmas tree when I was a boy
was beyond me now

Hercules would have failed at it

61

failed at what?
someone said

I looked in vain for a sign
I would see a sign

I don't suppose you remember me
someone said
we were friends when we were children
someone told me you were dying

it was becoming difficult to tell them apart
they were so many
the collective noun for ghosts is
a proliferation
they spring up everywhere
like forget-me-nots beside the road
like bluebells in woodland
like trees

I saw then that it was my mother
who knew a lot about nature

I'm not your mother
someone said

I saw then that it was my friend
who knew all the wild flowers
by their proper names
cow parsley
herb robert
touch-me-not

are you dead too?
I asked him
or would have done
if he had not been lost in the crowd

Neil Rathmell

THE RETRO TYPEWRITER

My father's Royalite typewriter,
the soundtrack of my childhood,
every evening at the kitchen table
the broken lullaby of cacophony
that kept the dark at bay.

My father, prelate of those sacred hours,
secluded from our ordinary world of family,
a long-haired maestro hitting the keys,
welcoming the ping of the margin bell
like the hospitable clinking of glasses.

I have treasured its bull-nosed contours,
keys faded and whorled from his fingerprints,
the sliding silver carriage release lever,
the leather case that never fully zipped,
buckled typebars in need of dental work.

Once he got angry and stormed out with
just a packed sponge bag and his typewriter.
My mother, with admirable presence of mind,
consulted the clock and put the kettle on. Now,
the typewriter sits as a sculpture in my lounge.

And I have fed into it one of the letters
he sent from Canada to his father: *Last Saturday*
marked the arrival of our winter snow.
It will not go away until the end of April.
And on the platen roller I've left exposed

what he said about me:
by when our wildest and naughtiest daughter
should have quietened down.
Love from us all.

Michael Henry

When she died and he moved on (which wasn't long),
the table came to me – disguised in its dismemberment –
lashed to his roof-rack like a mortarboard:
dark Belgian oak with heft enough
to seat a harmony of monks at bread.

For decades I housed it carelessly:
let summers bleach its grain to patchy wheat,
winters brand it with hot pans, kids stab
and scribble; cats hone sly claws.
And yes, that was a revenge of sorts.

He liked to brag he'd beaten down the price.
(Other beatings, he kept quiet about.)
Now the restorer finds its top is mere veneer
hiding thick chipboard. I'd scratched that surface,
sure; but not dug deep enough.

Susan Wallace

BOOMER

He has no home, he says, a man
who's sitting in a comfy chair
warm in a house he owns
its mortgage long paid-off.

He notes your disbelief
and understands his stance
is apt to cause offence
his generation blamed
for subsequent decline
in housing stock, their kids
priced out of homes themselves.

I have no home. The walls
the roof, the stuff I own
are not a substitute
for people that I loved
or didn't mind, liked well
enough to share a space
and pass the time of day.

His words are picked with care
– *back to my house*, he says
or names the town it's in
avoids the perjury
of calling it his home.
When he's away the dread
begins, his heart weighed down
with prospect of return.

Home was a time, he says
– *not a place, and not now.*

Stuart Handysides

SHELL

I would be happy to be a shell
Tumbled by the waves
Washed up on a distant shore
Picked up by a stranger
Who puts me to her ear
Listens to my story
Of travelling
Travelling the seas of the world
Beached on unknown lands
Lands of hope
Lands where people say
Welcome, yes, come ashore here
Lands where I want to stay
Forever.

Carole Thirlaway

LAMPEDUSA

All they bring is their spirit
enclosed somewhere, loosely

inside dark skins. Dark as the
night they emerge from, sodden

with the water of the boats baled
all the way from Africa. Faltering

throb of decrepit diesel engine,
oily water. Crammed, cold

in the sea wind. Only a dull
determined instinctual hope in their

tight numb chests. The certain
knowledge that the black gash of

the sea will be crossed to a new
life, or, if Fate wills it, they die.

Philip Dunkerley

HOME LEAVES

The house-bricks strain to straighten,
course by course in chiropractic air
along the wind's length.

The lime, the linden tree, waves goodbye
to wave on wave of leaves jetting home.
Low on chlorophyll, high on warm tones,
they guest on eddies, ride horizons
of their own making.

Turgid black fruits remain –
immobile phones
only starlings stoop to answer.

Above the finished fruited spurs,
above the wrist of church bells,
above the mordant steam
of charcoal, below the frosted
finger smoke of aviation oil
autumn leaves are jetting home.
They'll meet where all roads meet,
in furze, beyond the marsh, among cow parsley.

Philip Burton

BIRD STRIKE

1
Candle my shell, there's
the fledgling trapped inside.
It took a long time to chip my way out
featherless, bird beak wide, insatiable.

2
You know you're turning into a bird when:
you think the view would be better from higher up,
you stand on one leg and bathe in dust,
your skeleton becomes pneumatic, light,
you eat less, defy gravity.

3
Here's how they catch you –
lure you with whistles, a decoy, limed sticks.
One minute you're gorging on grain
then blind drowning
in a barrel of Armagnac.

The song of the ortolan contains the opening notes
of Beethoven's Fifth Symphony.

4
Stand amongst salicornia, waiting, silent,
another snipe hunt?

The courtship of snipe is wind
rushing through tail feathers,
a humming vibrato like a goat's bleat.

Roast in the oven and baste with butter,
layer the breasts in bacon,
serve on toast, baked in a potato or over a bed of sea beans.

5
Night, three blackbirds
circled Isadora's studio,
the next morning her children drowned.

Blackbirds divide up their fledglings.
The male usually cares for his group

for longer than the female
who leaves hers early
to start another brood.

6
Fairy Terns do not build a nest
but stick their eggs to a branch.
I suspect my parents were ostriches.

7
I am a quail plucked and scalded,
a pigeon rising in a clap of semaphore.
I am a widowed swan, a captive albatross,
a canary down a mine, a goose honking an alarm,
a starling, as the year turns,
weaving a dance of murmuration.

I am no-one's chick or hen or turtle dove
I am a chiffchaff calling out my own name.

Marion Hobday

Looking Towards Deansgate, York

BARGAINING WITH GOD
(*'A small bird will drop frozen dead from a bough without ever having felt sorry for itself.' D.H. Lawrence*)

Stoned and stunned by little people,
burying beak in its own neck,
the bird dies, dreaming and hoping,
though knowing nought of hopes or dreams,
yet feeling it and dreaming still, deep down, of dinosaur.
Then would it make those boys run so!

But The Lord has plans and grand design
and when he has gathered twenty souls:
Of perished robins frozen in snow,
swallows shot as they migrate,
starlings dead on chemical farms, famine-ravaged,
chaffinches, blackcaps, thrushes and doves, netted, glued and snared ...

This score collected, God then offers a deal:
One human life for all their separate little lives.
What will they choose to be – a boy or a girl?
But if in prisons kept or starved or bombed, they twitter,
putting ghostly heads together,
what then, after all, would be the point?

Clive Donovan

A woman points at the pavement.
I follow her gaze, and there
you sit. Sash-cord tail backed up
against blacked shop-front and its
unnoticed gap.

I haven't seen a rat for years.
Not since my father shook
a dead one in my face. His joke.
I wet myself.

We wait it out, you and I.
Time slows to an
animal moment.
Eyeball to eyeball.

Unsure left paw hovers, pink in mid-air.
The question we both ask is:
How did I end up here?
Tiny brain clicks. You turn slowly,
heave your potato body towards
home. Safety of the dark.

I remain, stranded in the light.

Fiona Theokritoff

Unfortunately this small puffer fish is dull almost to the point of obscurity
but even in modern relationships it is customary for the man to pop the question.

To grab a female's attention he does something that defies belief
disclosing financial status, career prospects and any expectations.

His only tools are fins and a plan of mathematical perfection,
the procedure begins with a visit to the father of the girl.

He ploughs the sand breaking it into the finest of particles,
consider a pre-nuptial agreement – marriage may be fragile.

Shells aren't rubbish to be removed
engagement rings always carry a stone.

He decorates the ridges of his construction
rubies, sapphires and emeralds are most popular.

He can't rest for a moment, working 24 hours a day
one month's salary is what he lays out on a ring.

A final tidy up and the masterpiece is complete
commemorate the occasion with a portrait photograph.

Nowhere in nature is there a construction as complex as this
make an announcement in the Telegraph Marriage column.

If this doesn't get him noticed, nothing will.

Anne Symons

(Note: This 'found' poem uses words from David Attenborough's
commentary on 'Life Story' (BBC One, November 2014) and text from
Debrett's *Guide to Etiquette and Modern Manners* (September 1996))

CHAOS
GEOMETRY
DELIRIUM

In Space it seems
There is no place
For rectangles
Angles apparently
Are of purely
Earthly interest

Likewise squares and oblongs
Rhombi and trapezia
Everything out there
Is spiral curved and circular
Stellar bodies in their orbits
Have little time for corners as a concept

So how come here
We're wall-to-wall
Bricks and boxes cubes
And chocolate bars
Something somewhere is amiss
All observations tell us this

We're moving through a vast morass
Of senseless rotational
Helter skelter chaos
The Universe in short is in a spin
So surely this is where Sapiens comes in
To bring a measure of order and of purpose

To implement a non-entropic state
Of Pythagorean harmony
A haven for harmless quadrilaterals
And unsurprising parallelograms
And halt once and for all
The dreadful centrifugal maelstrom

We'll take our destiny in both hands
And turn this frankly botched concoction
That is the Cosmos
Into something static something stable
Something nice and normal something sensible
It is the only logical solution

For now that Man is specifically perfect
We are the only God we need
Digitally enhanced today

If we should draw tomorrow
An existential parallel
No-one will be the wiser

Omniscient omnipotent
We'll first abolish physics
Subtracting temporal from spatial
To create a novel symmetry
Making galaxies safe at last
For Euclidian geometry ...

... Then at that point
One of our number
That I do not recognize
Stops me 'Unless
It has already happened'
'And who exactly' I enquire
'Might you be?'

Paul Durrant

NORMALITY

You sample a population,
measure each identical part,
use Sturges' Rule, or Scott's,
if the numbers are large,
to create a histogram
then check the assumption
that it's a Normal Distribution.

When an outlier
is found,
test with Grubb's
or Dixon's Q,
to determine if that one data point that stands out
is too different
to fit the hypothesis,
an opinion,
cloaked in jargon,
statistics,
that could be
me and you.

Patrick Druggan

I sift through memories of our shared benches and chemistry lectures for
Avogadro's Number. We were bored boys then, talked of travelling the
world, dreamed of being poets. Our revolution against science written in
student pads, in the secret rosary kept in your pocket.

I find it in a reference book, heavy as a bible, from 1968 that says it was

6.0225×10^{23}

It smells of old age and laboratories, as if carried across the Taklamakan,
spent cold nights in caravansarai smoked by their fires, like Russian teas,
through the Ferghana valley, to Samarkand and the plains where the Syr
Darya once met the Aral Sea, now empty as the wind.

Everything we rely on changes with time
even the constants.

I check the standard for SI units from 2019, to calculate the current of ion
stream hitting a Faraday Plate. It's changed to

6.0221×10^{23}

You send a message from Colombia, where you've lived for thirty years.
It tells me your world is flat, with a video of the dark sun and star
projections. Your page is full of conspiracy theorists, Australia First,
prayers to Saint Dympna, and a suffering Christ.

Patrick Druggan

REMEDIAL CHEMISTRY

The teacher was too young
And didn't take the register –
So I called myself Jack.

She saw only inconvenience
Within a class of outright defiance,
Gassing itself on the Bunsens.

We copied blackboard chalk –
The chemical equation of stupidity
And added tits and cocks.

Where X equals loneliness
And Y equals boredom,
I was a formula for trouble.

But her code was kindness –
Her notation was inclusive,
Expecting me to be honest
About adolescent molecules
And acne faced electrons.

My real name was adoration,
But she never worked that out.

Robin Lindsay Wilson

DAVID GOSLING

When he multiplied two
and three-digit numbers in his head
some of us gasped, others just stared
at him open-mouthed, then at Sir

who smiled, raised his eyebrows,
but didn't ask how he did it,
as if he were a magician
and shouldn't reveal his secrets.

Sitting behind him,
I studied the back of his head,
and thought of that picture
Miss Toklas showed us in Art:

a labyrinth of staircases
meeting at impossible angles,
infinite flights that must
disappear into the clouds.

We worked in silence.
Whenever I looked up at Goz
he was gazing out of the window,
his mind somewhere else.

John Lynch

TEENAGE LOVE LETTER
(For Lilliana)

Remember my love letter embarrassing itself as poetry?
'Your freckles are ecstasy to me from your sweet
cheeks' or 'O, how the space between your front teeth
is the gap of beauty.' You laughed, even then, oh so rightly.

Remember the day of your tattoo? Down to a 'dungeon'
off the Portobello Road. The tattooist boasting of
inking the Sex Pistols; his punk rock fables more
gruelling than the needle. After, in the park, remember?

Us, puffing weed clouds into shapes of eight while
fathoming if bees, stoned, would pollinate. And I,
fumbling and grappling like a drunken wrestler to plant
you a kiss, as you followed the butterfly rising into the Sun.

Michael Wyndham

FIRST BITE OF THE BARD

The centipedes have arrived. Coach-loads
of raw sixteen-year-olds being put through
the mixer of their first hands-on
experience of Shakespeare.

Under the *dirigiste* eye of teachers
they settle in the upper stalls,
sniff the nail varnish newness
of a pass-the-parcel programme.

Appraising a photograph of Romeo,
one girl says, 'He's got a nice bum.'
Her teacher, finger on puckered lips,
tries to *unwhisper* it. Is he remembering

his first trip to Stratford
being told off for 'making eyes at Mary Ure'?
A last creak of lacquered pages,
like tulips, before curtain-rise.

The centipedes like it
when Romeo thunders in on a motorbike
and when his crash-helmet doubles
as a hair-dryer for Juliet.

A teacher explains to them
this is called anachronism and it goes
in a Chinese whisper down the rows.
Drinks on the balcony in the interval.

Swans with belled out wings ruffle
the reflections from the lights of narrowboats
moored at the side of the River Avon.
'The performance will resume in two minutes.'

Front-of-house shuffles into place. Like cards.
A teacher uses his ticket as dental tape.
Something has wedged there.
And won't come out. Like words.

Michael Henry

AT THE LIGHTS

I see Rachel French; hardly
changed from twenty years ago
when her squeals drew the class

around her desk by the window
where a mirror, at an angle
in a tray of water, reflected

the colours of the spectrum
onto a piece of white card;
her joy undimmed

by my attempt to explain
how light rays refract.
A rainbow! I made a rainbow!

she shouted, so loud children
on their way to the hall stopped
to stare through the open door;

her eyes shining, and that big smile;
the same one she gives me now
as she crosses in front of my car.

I wave as I pull away,
chuffed with how her face lit up
when she saw me.

John Lynch

THE PIGEON COOP

It was to be my first holiday. Mom had stated firmly that we could not afford a family holiday, so she had arranged for each of us to stay with a different relative. That is how I came to stay with aunt Thea. *Old* aunt Thea, never married, living with aunt Mona and uncle Frederick, who were not even a real aunt and uncle as far as I could make out. Thea was the real aunt, and she lived with the two of them.

It was a change alright: three small rooms in a tiny house, living room, kitchen and one small bedroom. It was a wonder they had offered to have me at all. Three old people lived here, three lives so firmly wedded to their routines that they unrolled wordlessly, and to me, mysteriously. They presented me with a new language of living, one that I needed to decode and learn.

None of them ever had children, so there were no toys, nor any sign of anybody ever having been young. But there was something else, a sense of welcome that quickly made me feel the center of their universe. Small gifts showed up out of nowhere, little indulgences were offered; a dish would be filled with candy just for me, accompanied by a quiet encouragement to help myself to whatever I pleased. Suddenly I needed to know what *I* wanted to do, what *I* felt like eating, heady and, at times, difficult questions to answer. While I found my bearings, their quiet routines eddied around me, and their personalities slowly began to separate and become distinct.

Clearly, aunt Thea with her important job, her education, her elegant and expensive wardrobe, had the say. Yet, the small house, I found out, had belonged to aunt Mona's parents. Aunt Mona, always dressed in black, was partially deaf and often wore a scarf tied around her head and under her chin to protect her ears, her hair was gathered in a bun at the nape of her neck. Her figure was small and delicate. She was always doing for others and seemed to understand their needs before they recognized them themselves. Self-effacing and observant, kind and mouse-like, I only learned years later that she hardly ever left the house, and that aunt Thea and uncle Frederick executed a protective dance around her.

Uncle Frederick worked in the steel mill in this town owned by steel barons. Taciturn, he hoarded words as if reluctant to squander them in the daily give-and-take of living. To me he seemed a huge man whose oversized, calloused hands swung loosely at his sides. He had been working hard since a young age. Surreptitiously I took in his plain manners, and his, to my ears, truncated sounding speech. I also noted the way he reached for his cap the moment he was finished eating before exiting through the backdoor to be with his pigeons.

He kept carrier pigeons, a whole coop of cooing, flapping birds in the loft of a barn-like structure in the back yard. He would end up staying there for hours and had to be called back in person at mealtimes. During his absence, the routine in the house would close comfortingly around female concerns. Soft laughter erupted and followed aunt Thea and aunt Mona, who, it seemed, continued an on-going dialogue that seemed strange, and, at times, incomprehensible to me.

I knew the part of the story, the part where aunt Thea's house had been bombed during the war and aunt Mona, only a distant acquaintance at the time, had offered her temporary shelter. Now, decades later, their arrangement had become honoured by time, as each of them had found their niche in that confined space of a living room, kitchen and one small bedroom.

The living room was as overstuffed as the bedroom, each doily in place, a room used only when company came. The kitchen was the true center of their universe. Here, menus were planned, daily occurrences re-lived, and tea was drunk at table at all hours. I was surprised to learn that uncle Frederick slept on the hard, horsehair stuffed couch in the corner of the kitchen, surrounded by rows and rows of framed photos of his prize pigeons along two walls; their genealogy and achievements spelled out in fine print below their tripod feet; and I would wonder how this big man fitted on that narrow couch and how this could be his bed.

I, on the other hand, slept in the center of aunt Thea's and aunt Mona's bed, in the place where the two marital beds were joined and where one usually found a cold and drafty gap. They had taken care of that by rolling up and flattening a blanket so that I could lie there like "the Princess of the week" that I had become. To my right slept aunt Thea, who warranted an extra small pillow, lace-edged, for the small of her head, to my left lay aunt Mona, plain cotton all the way.

Part of my life with them included an early afternoon nap in bed, "… you don't have to sleep, but you should have a rest …" the two of them would chime, leaving me to trace the marbled veins in the heavy fixture on the ceiling and follow the gentle billowing of the white curtains. Now and then I caught a glimpse of the narrow garden, a garden that conformed strictly to the narrowness of the house itself. I could make out the gentle amorous cooing of the pigeons on the roof of the coop and wondered, why did uncle Frederick not sleep with his wife in the big marital bed, in the bedroom that was theirs? Was aunt Thea really in charge, or was aunt Mona the true center of the arrangement? Who was married to whom? Was uncle Frederick all he seemed? Did he really live in the pigeon coop as the women insisted? Too many questions, too much I didn't know and couldn't ask; sleep seemed easier and less demanding; eventually I must have surrendered, letting myself drift to the inside of the pigeon coop:

I could feel the sun-dried wooden rungs of the ladder under my bare feet as I climbed towards the open hatch. Inside, I found a world of floating feathers and a continuous, insistent cooing. The ululating sound of constant begetting filled my ears. The light, filled with a thousand motes of dust, threw broad bands of sunshine, like parts of the milky way, across the wide floorboards; all I could make out was uncle Frederick's dark shape cradling a pigeon in his enormous hands while he carefully banded it, to identify it as his own, and to ensure its ultimate return.

Barbara Ponomareff

LEVELLED UP

Let me be clear, Ossett needs fewer books
and the library is better in a basement.
The 5pm drinkers outside Moody's are fighting fit.
That Community Policing poster does the trick.
The DIY shop's knives, sledgehammer
and fertiliser will be used responsibly.
That staffy is a softy.

CCTV MONITORING and
24-HOUR SECURITY PATROL are Good Signs.
The roof where the flashing was lifted
and patched with blue plastic, loose tiles and a plank
will be of little interest next Saturday night.
Ossett sees no substance abuse
or mental illness.
The mesh barriers have moved themselves.

The Health Centre was not meant to last
more than thirteen years.
The weeds hiding the car park and entrance ramp
are urban re-wilding.
Those who used the Day Centre
took up their beds and walked,
those with dementia found their way to Wakefield
and those who struggle to walk are happy
to stay in.

Julia Deakin

I DO NOT LOOK FOR VERDANT FIELDS

Morning, bright as a freshly-laid egg:
dawnlight, ecstatic birdsong, angel's breath
blowing clouds across the sky – and demons
waiting silently to pounce, to devour the day,
to suck love out of the universe.

The Black Dog stirs, bares his yellow teeth;
grey shrouds obliterate the sun; a heavy stone
falls and settles in the belly's basement –
a gross intruder. And this every day, cruel
and relentless as creeping cancer.

What spiteful gods decree such suffering:
is it arbitrary or deserved, a punishment
for past sins? Or is it merely a misalignment
of the stars, a chemical storm in the brain?
I neither know nor care – I seek only sweet relief.

I do not look for verdant fields, music melting
like warm honey in receptive ears, or the silver
siren songs of distant stars. No, I would settle gladly
for a good night's sleep and waking in the morning
with the stone in my stomach dissolved to gravel.

Bill Fitzsimmons

I'd been working all day in my pyjamas, as one does, when the doorbell went. It was my neighbour. Not the English students who offered me home-made brownies on their first day then were never seen again, nor the curmudgeonly gaunt old guy with a hooked nose who asked me if I knew where the building's TV aerial was (I didn't), nor the nice plump lady who once asked if I had seen her cat anywhere on the landing (I went out with her laying out bowls of ripped up chicken slices around the building to entice the cat, later found safely hiding in a gap under the lady's bathroom sink).

No, it was the scatty, stressed and stressful neighbour who lived directly down the stairs from me, who had once shrieked at me over the intercom – yes, she went down to the close on the street to do this – for having purchased and then used repeatedly in the mornings a very expensive waste-of-money exercise machine at the height of lockdown, which, to be fair, did turn out to be height of loud squeakiness.

Now, here she stood again – the first time we'd spoken since that little episode. I was extremely cognisant of the fact I was wearing pyjamas. My neighbour asked me, in that both pleading and demanding way of hers, if it was me making that noise.

I asked her what noise, and she paused and held her finger in the air for several seconds, and said, you were making it a minute ago, and I said, I've just been working at my desk for hours, pretty much in silence unless you count occasionally boiling the kettle for a cuppa. And she said, finger still poised like a conductor waiting to begin a performance, so it wasn't you? And I said, *what* wasn't me? I haven't heard anything. And then her finger banged the air. *There*, she said. *That noise.* Do you hear it? I told her I couldn't hear a thing and she frowned. Maybe it's someone up the stairs or someone else on my floor, I offered. She said, but it's coming from right on top of me. I thought but didn't say, *oo-er, madam.*

She looked confused, frazzled and rather pale. I recalled I thought she worked in healthcare or perhaps social care, although that may only be based on how hard she used to bang the pans downstairs when they did the clap for carers. This time she held up a whole hand as she said, *There*, again, can you hear that? I asked her what it sounded like, and she said, like banging, or grinding, and I thought but didn't say, *oo-er, madam.*

From the computer at my desk next door, I heard the ping of my work instant messaging app going off and felt the tug of my desk like I was on the end of a fishing line. I don't know what to tell you, I can't hear anything, I said, and she seemed really rattled now, saying, how can't you hear it? It's still going right now. It's relentless, it's maddening. It hasn't stopped since morning. I tried a joke. Maybe it's a ghost, I said. This, it turned out, was unwise. Is that a joke? she asked, looking crushed, despondent. I said, yeah, obviously. And she said, well, it's not funny, and I said, sorry. For an awful moment, I thought she was going to cry, and I was almost going to invite her in for a cup of tea, until I heard my app pinging again. I'm sorry, I said, that's work calling. Duty calls. Good luck tracking that noise down, though.

She looked at me distractedly, somehow contriving to nod and shake her head at the same time. Slowly, with an apologetic smile, I shut the door on her.

At the door, I stood and listened until I heard her footsteps flumping on the stairs – whether up or down, I couldn't be sure. Once the noise had subsided, I took a breath and went into the boiler room. I hitched the chair up onto the spare disused coffee table I kept there and carefully stood on it, then knocked on the attic hatch door above the boiler.

I gently pushed the door until it opened completely and flipped onto the other side, and there was the little alien who had taken up residence there, with its pinky-red scales like a lobster, wearing a tiny pair of goggles and wielding a tiny welder's torch emitting a tiny blue flame, various tiny tools attached to his twelve flailing pink limbs.

I said, you need to keep it down up there, my neighbour from downstairs is onto you and she stresses me out. It started chattering in its own strange tongue, a very fast-paced, nasal, oscillating speech that reminded me of special effects sounds you get on an electric guitar pedal, interposed with a mind-boggling array of clicking and popping sounds of infinite textures.

Remember, I can't understand you, I said, do the thing where you beam your thoughts directly into my mind.

So the alien did, and it said, into my mind, *Peace, Nathaniel, my work shan't take much longer, and then I will have fixed the components of my divine engine that were damaged in my most unfortunate crash, and after that, my ship shall be ready for flight once more. As I previously intimated, I can offer you payment by way of taking you into my ship and to an extraordinary voyage through the stars, showing you the great wonders and civilisations throughout the cosmos, or, as previously intimated, I can pay you a large sum of money in your local currency.* And I said, I'll take the money. Just try to keep it down, mate.

Dan Vevers

AUDIT

A woman is woken by a boom – as if from an explosion – but nobody is panicking or running on the street. It seems she is the only person who heard it.

She tries to identify it, searching the National Archives of the Audible, listening till she's dizzy to blasts and detonations, but nothing approximates the sound that she recalls.

An audio editor tries to recreate it from her description. Five attempts – he gets as near as he can; a range of peaks that dance across his digital screen. He puts it on a memory stick for her to take away, like a surgeon handing over a gallstone in a bottle.

~

There's a ringing in my ears.

In fact, more like a rushing than a ringing. And a clock ticking somewhere – very fast – and this singing which suggests a field of particles, scintillating, shifting around, close-packed and filled with light, while the beat of the clock-tick behind them is dark.

The volume is surging and diminishing, but mostly surging. Such hurry in that clock and the sound overall, persistent like the purple image on the eye after too-long looking at a bulb that's too bright.

A presence to which I am – however – reconciled.

~

Six in the morning. I open the back door and step into the yard. The sky – blue already – is scored across with white, and reverberates with one thrumming roar after another.

A buddleia plant on the roof next-door-but-one is coming into bloom; twin tall stems in a ragged clump of foliage. Steam clouds up from the wall of that house – lit by the sun – but the vent is in shadow, so it appears to be welling up from nowhere. Above, the vapour trails turn indistinct and powdery.

Things that can go wrong on a plane: metal fatigue in the wings or the fuselage, inadequate pressurization in the cabin, a pilot with a grudge; an elderly passenger, apparently untroubled, who announces on touchdown, 'I don't know who I am and I don't know where I'm going!'

Mary Michaels

RESURRECTION

We practised taxidermy on that puppet
you bought, stripped it to ventricles and bone,
chopped the head with your wooden sword.

Set it on a platter, head glowering back at us
like John the Baptist, witnessing our wrongs.
We dissected the long aorta, the bloody heart

mushed them in a bowl. We dirtied our fingers
in secret crevasses, ripped nails from each hand,
argued over which limb to unpick, how to stop

the insistence of the voice box calling
                                    Hello, Hello.

Lynn Valentine

Jen and her doll Pete got on the bus to go home after another children's party sparkling with chaotic jollity. Pete wanted to talk to the driver but he threatened to charge him full fare, grumpy sod, so up they went at the front on top – I kept Pete quiet on the way home cos I needed to think, I was wondering about the child with the speech problem and whether we could help, but I didn't want to say anything to Pete until I'd thought it through because he gets over-excited – When the children are having fun Jen says sometimes I get carried away and don't think what I'm saying which is true, I just don't – There was a recommendation and we got asked to gig for a birthday and it was the sister of the child who couldn't speak or wouldn't, so it was a job and that's better for Pete and I didn't have to worry about offering to help or interfering or Pete being too forward – After we'd done our little routine Jen let me chat to the boy who felt so vulnerable, afraid to start words he couldn't finish, to make sounds that came out wrong or clashed so violently with the droning in his head. And what other than a numbing anxiety, a sense of being gowned and brought to slaughter, could he know at a party where all the others giggled and bickered and squealed and screamed as if there was no such clashing or droning or doubt, and him dispensable in the rites around him. I was just talking to the boy just him, in the corner, and saying how sometimes what I said didn't make sense or came out wrong and sometimes I wanted to say something but couldn't or Jen wouldn't let me – Then the boy who couldn't speak told Pete his name was Peter too and they smiled and made up a poem about a boy called Pete with enormous feet that hated meat, and laughed because it sounded like it was the feet that hated meat, so there had to be another verse to untangle that, and the party was going on by itself and then it was about a hen called Jen who lived in a den and they wept or Jen did anyway for sure – And then after, me and Jen got on the bus and smiled in our silence all the way home.

Kevin Armor Harris

The Minster & St Michael le Belfry

THE BLUE SOCKS

live for tomorrow
they hide in the back of the drawer

though friendly with the other socks
they cower before shoes

they cling to dryer sheets and fuzzy
blankets

they are quiet
they have little to do until chosen

they deny knees and struggle
to pass over ankles

you may forget them

until they are pulled from that space
behind the laundry hamper

they are modest
about their usefulness

they might even
come clean

Kelley Jean White

Music and Secrets

There are the secrets that lovers have, and the secrets of husband and wife; there are professional secrets, the secrets of the skilled. Every musician has their own, which are shared only with the instrument they play. The viola player has more than most maybe, and the viola seems to hold secrets of its own. There are no secrets in music, only those of music itself, which may always remain a mystery. They are understood by everyone as they listen, but no-one can explain them.

The Audience

They look forward, each of them, to something different, something individual and very personal to them. Their thoughts and memories hang in the air about them, almost as if they too are preparing, just as the orchestra tune their instruments. To hear a favourite piece played once more; to see a famous performer, or a new, unknown one; for a few hours of pleasure and delight, even to escape a life where there is none; to remind them of an earlier time perhaps, with a companion who is no longer with them. To remember, to forget. And to feel in this way all that they might feel in their everyday lives, but shaped and beautifully painted in sound and colour.

Whatever they hear or see, they will experience different things in the concert. And they will know the pleasure and excitement of music as it is played – fifty, a hundred skilled musicians, working together, each one as important as the other, and the instruments themselves, all the craft of their making, wood, gold, silver: art and skill come together, joined together just to this purpose – as if life might somehow always be like this.

The Conductor

As he lifts his arms he is all eyes, all nerve, all will. His hands control and command, they act and speak. They are perfection, those strong, strange hands, the flat backs beautifully carved, the wrists powerful but fine, the complex wiring of veins.

Jewelled cufflinks flash in the light.

He works only with the finest musicians, the most beautiful and youthful, his pride allows nothing else. And these two are amongst the finest – the violinist his own young wife (she is his third wife) and the viola-player, this latest striking young star whom everyone wishes to engage now.

He regards the young man critically, assessingly – he has not worked with him before. And his gaze flits freely over the violinist's skin, as his fingers have so often done: the memory in his fingertips.

But there are age spots on the backs of those hands, and the knuckles have become more prominent. Whenever he can, he leans back for support against the podium.

The Violinist
She raises her violin – its soft lines and graceful shape reflect her own; the delicate shell of her ears is like the scroll of the instrument. Her long dark hair is caught up at the back of her neck. Her arms and shoulders are smooth and soft like a child's.

She dares not look at his eyes, she watches only his hands, manicured and handsome … the fear of them … But there are things he cannot control now – he can beat out time in lines and gestures, but the music, and its meaning, slips between the bars and away from him.

The Viola Player
It is the viola that gives its character to the piece. Its tone is darker, husky, and veiled, as if it were heard through muslin; but each viola, each player, has their own sound. It is harder to play than the violin, especially in its highest register, because of its greater size, its broader shoulders – though there is no one length or shape for the viola.

But its strings are tuned a little higher in this work, *scordatura*, and this brighter sound makes it a more equal partner to the violin, and its music is equally difficult.

He is young, this player, ambitious for himself and his viola. He loves its strangeness, its awkwardness, the fact that there is no standard sound – it is in every way his own instrument, he has made it his own. He tries to make every performance different.

He has not worked with this conductor before, though he is acquainted with his wife.

He raises the viola to his chin.

The Composer
The viola was his own preferred instrument. If he was not at the piano this time, performing one of his own concertos maybe, he could sit amongst the other players, in the heart of the sound and the texture. He was no longer a child prodigy, though still a young man, only twenty-three, small and slight, but he was travelling to different countries, to France and Germany, learning new ways of writing and performing, experimenting with different forms and styles, a larger scale. Not long after completing this piece he finally left his narrow, stifling employment in Salzburg, and moved to the capital, to Vienna.

His music is full of sweetness and silver grace, but there can be dark waters beneath a silver surface; he can twist the heart and the soul suddenly with just a few notes. And he came to prefer the darker tones – the clarinet rather than the flute or the oboe, the horn rather than the trumpet: the viola.

No other composers at this time wrote for it in this way, he seemed to understand its character, its roughness, its acquaintance somehow with darkness and forbidden emotion.

With this piece he found something new to say, something borrowed from a later time, as if he is drawing back a curtain to show this different, darker world. There is sadness and grief – he was grieving for the death of his mother at this time – but as such a young man, where in himself did he find this sense of the tragic and the hopeless? Why these two players, why this dialogue between them, why this music?

As a composer, he is concerned with technical matters, with form and structure – how do these other things find their way between the lines and into the sounds that we hear? What did he know or understand of what he wrote in this work?

Why? ... How? ...

Violin and Viola

There had been very little time for rehearsal. There was a problem in the hall, the lighting not adequate apparently, the conductor creating an unnecessary storm about the matter. So he chose to work only on the opening of the piece, then a section of the short finale. The second movement, the heart of the work, he hardly touched, speaking to the players only generally of mood and speed. He could take more time then with the other pieces to be performed – a short overture, and the long symphony that would form the second half of the concert.

He is unwell and in pain, as often now, leaning back against the rail, sparing himself. But his eyes still speak power and control.

The young soloists enter the stage; there is applause and great anticipation – they are a handsome couple. He wears a silken shirt and wide-flared trousers; her flowing dress is of the same dark colour. The concerto has a grand, majestic opening, almost like a symphony, and the soloists emerge together from this background, with long held notes clear and firm as the mist of sound melts from around them, almost as if they were special beings formed from it, made strong and shining as the sun breaks clear.

It is like this sometimes with love, when it happens – everything else is only background. And it is about these two only now: the music is in their hands in every way; it is their space, their time. And she feels that she is safe now, in this music, safe, for once.

She can see the conductor's eyes change.

The slow movement might come almost from an opera, though without words it has more meaning. The music is heavy and slow, it leans and limps. The violin is tentative and uncertain, questioning; the viola replies, with understanding and consolation, then takes the questions further, questioning the questions, the phrases longer, risking more, rising higher, higher even than the violin.

It is the music that leads them – they cannot play the piece in any other way, without emotion, or only with pretence – they are professionals, they play with all the feeling and the understanding that is needed. But there is more now, something unexpected, something unaccountable, that perhaps they hardly knew or understood themselves before this time. Something they cannot express in any other way,

They do not need the conductor here. He can only follow them.

Conductor and orchestra halt for the Cadenza. It is a long one, written by the composer himself. Conductor, orchestra, audience are all forgotten, the soloists are alone and free now, lost in tenderness and grief, in hopeless hope, their voices interweaving like longing and loss. She speaks of her loneliness, her fear of her husband, she speaks of his eyes, his hands, so strong still in spite of his years; and of her dream of another's arms around her, of a different love, a different strength. He speaks of her hair, of her skin, her frailty, her need, he speaks of his pity for her and his passion. They ask Why, and How? and If?

Their eyes are locked together, darkness and silver light, they speak also. It is personal, and private, not meant for any audience.

The Conductor
He did not foresee everything that would happen; he is powerless for once.

He can only accompany the soloists. Of course he will do it well, as he does everything well; he is a musician above all, it is his reputation as much as theirs which might be judged. But at the end of the Cadenza he stands motionless, as if he is elsewhere, in a place he does not recognise. He gazes downwards, his baton laid back on the stand, his hands shaking. The leader of the orchestra glances at him – and after a moment she takes the orchestra to the end, they play the final melancholy bars alone, as if they are pulling across a last curtain.

He is too proud to admit even the possibility of what he has seen, but he is too fine a musician to miss its message, or to ignore it. He suspects, but he cannot really believe it to be true. He needs a beautiful young wife – he needs her body at night, her youth, her assistance, in the day, he will need her to care for him as he ages further. Her glamour: his mortality. He knows that she fears him, but she fears too that if she leaves him her career might suffer.

He thinks of all these things, though he has no proof, he can make no reproaches. But as he listens to their playing, it is clear, the proof is there.

The Audience
They see, but they do not understand. They are enraptured by the playing, by the sympathy between the players, they know there has been something exceptional: 'A wonderful performance!' – 'So deeply felt', they comment later. 'Almost as if they were in love themselves!' – 'The

conductor so moved by their playing!' Perhaps they thought at times of their own lives, of loves come and gone.

But perhaps it is the orchestra who are the true audience, watching, understanding, knowing: spell-bound.

The Finale

The finale is a whirlwind, and the conductor takes it fast: laughter and blown leaves, champagne and lace, sunlit fountains. 'Forget, forget everything! It is only the moment that matters!'

Maybe, perhaps; probably? But nothing was real, nothing was true. It was one story only, amongst all those that this music holds.

Meaningless, empty, it is gone.

Then, later, dark streets, trains, the taxis home, the hotel rooms ...

Frances Thimann

(Note: the piece referred to here is the Sinfonia Concertante for Violin and Viola, K 364, by Mozart.)

THE GO-BETWEEN
(from *Woman Writing a Letter with her Maid* by Vermeer)

I stand just here, my dress falling just so, across
the marble harlequins. Sir is very particular about that.
He wanted to see my fingers on my arm.
She didn't like that. Or the blue silk sash he draped on me.

But I am the shadow and she is the light.
I listen to the muffled sounds from the Herengracht,
the scratch of her quill. I can hear her breathing hard,
half-smile on her face, demure but furtive.

Her seal and the wax have slid from the table;
she is so engrossed in her task.
I shall retrieve them when she bids me; also
the guide for letter-writing, her ruse.

When it's sealed and safe, I will go out through the back,
deliver it to the address I know. While I wait, I flirt
with his manservant. Those eyes tell me all I need to know.
No need for letters.

Fiona Theokritoff

BROCKEN SPECTRES

The first haunted my footsteps
balancing up a ridge in the Rhinog range,
a flicker of movement at the corner of my eye
that stopped when I stopped
to scan shifting banks of cloud,
lifting, dispersing, coalescing among
peaks golden with early morning sunlight,
seeking some unexpected fellow-traveller.
Turning to move on, he was back
lifting his arm as I lifted mine
to shade my eyes for another look –
my stalking shadow, haloed with light.

Others followed me across the Alps
but never had I seen a brocken spectre
look so much like a rainbow as yesterday's
cast on a wide sea of cloud that lapped
the rocky shores of islanded Welsh summits
or rose to inundate them in obscurity.
Not just a glow, but a double rainbow
arched over our two shadows, dark traces
there at the heart of that shining spectrum
splashed upon the brimming cloud-base.

And though this was no Ararat
I took it as an omen that
despite our broken spars, splintered timbers,
often caulked but still springing leaks,
our sails tattered and patched, and a crew
that's mostly jumped ship after a voyage
becalmed at times in doldrum wastes of water
or tempest-tossed, close-hauled past wrecking headlands
arriving now at shores seething with gunboats,
the hold emptied of endangered species,
two by two or not;
                          despite all that
there just might be more rainbows.

Dave Wynne-Jones

ATTACHMENT

up to my neck with it
this aloneness flips me
winded, wounded, supine
a little thrashing beetle
somehow still at the mercy
of you, abrupt instigator
of life, fantasies, departures
before you left this time
I could barely watch
you gaze into the pool of
all-too delirious self-regard,
only now, without your
complexion to ridicule,
I ghost from room to room
as if I was made to tread,
to stew, in the residue
of your never presence
craving the same return
I swore off just a matter
of hours ago, which I
believe is the definition
of an ingenious trap
not here with/out you

Alex Rourke

A pile for 'him' and a pile for 'her'.
Twenty years and it's come to this.

The mahogany music stand – 'his'.
The mini pyramid ornaments – 'hers'.
The toaster – 'his'.
The porcelain chopsticks – 'not sure'.
Plates from his intrusive mother – 'Who cares?!'

The origami child coiled in the corner – 'theirs'.
Some things can never be unshared.

Carmella de Keyser

ABOUT YOU

Can I think about you at the start of the day
when you've snoozed your alarm and you've ended up late,
when the overcast sky is a uniform grey
and the scales kick you off in disgust at your weight?

Can I note that your car's been a target for birds
and describe how the wind makes a mess of your hair?
Can I know that you've damaged your heel on the curb
and you never forget your ex-husband's affair?

Can I hereby acknowledge your luck with the lights,
how they all turn to red as they watch you draw near,
how your miscreant gearbox is anxious to fight
your frustrated endeavours selecting a gear?

Can I tailgate, unnoticed, at quarter to nine
when there's no one to make you your first cup of tea,
get a load of your screensaver's tragic design
that's a bucket-list montage of things you won't see?

May I clarify here that your boss is a twat
who converses in nothing but fatuous guff?
I should buy him a mannequin's arse he can pat
(though he doesn't need more midlife crisis-ey stuff).

And perhaps I'll just wait here till quarter past five
when your colleagues all leave at the end of the day
in a joyous return to their adequate lives
to their slow cooker dinners and cheap Beaujolais.

Do you mind if I follow you back through your door
and observe with a frown that you're cooking for one,
see the value brand wine that you're too quick to pour
while defiantly chasing an echo of fun?

May I hear that your phone doesn't bother to ring
as you're sitting alone with some shit on TV,
note un-manicured nails on the fingers that cling
to the comfortless arm of your threadbare settee?

May I stare at the washing that needs to be done
and the bookcase that's coated with dust in the hall?

Dream Catcher 50

Can I flick through the novel you haven't begun
and assume I've the rights of a fly on the wall?

For I'm wondering whether there's some common ground
in the winding of roads and the turning of bends,
if the threads of our fates could be gently unwound
in a way that could mean we'll be more than just friends

Chris Scriven

NOWADAYS

I'd say that, nowadays, love has it tough,
it's elbowed out by stupid other stuff;
the nuisance tasks, the nine to five, the bills …
It's lost between The Range and Trago Mills.
Love's not retained its place within the queue,
it's dropped right off our list of things to do.

In unobtrusive quietude love waits
beneath the laundry, under dirty plates.
Submissively, it's pushed before a broom
that sweeps it to the corners of the room,
a half-forgotten, disregarded friend
whose patience may be almost at an end.

Regretfully, love's been partitioned off,
it's with the relics weighing-down the loft,
it's stashed behind the mower in the shed,
love's duvet's in the drawer beneath the bed.
Once instinct, now a habit almost stopped,
a photo time has mercilessly cropped.

Love's learnt the safety protocol of flight
when pins are pulled that detonate a fight.
Inherently unable to take sides,
love knows to duck, to leave the room, to hide,
to camouflage itself against the wall
and silently observe the rising gall.

But right between the conflict and the kiss,
it lets us know it's there, it still exists
and, secretly, I hope love has the edge
on anger, hope that it will drive a wedge
between our vast and twinned tectonic plates
of bitterness and blame, of rage and hate.

Chris Scriven

GORDALE SCAR

Looking at that great gash
in the rock outcrop
you'd think a giant's axe
had been at work.

Solid rock splits.
The shock of it rips into the viscera.
His words were sledgehammer blows
that broke the glass in the front door
she slammed it so hard.
Looking down into the rift
the fissured walls look torn and raw.

But no, it was the slow friction,
the flowing stream eating
into the limestone
over millions of years that did for it.

How small humans seem
on the grassy slopes below
in the minutes of the day
as they love and hate, suffer
the slow trickle of disagreements,
betrayals, disappointments.

While unnoticed in the pools
small pebbles metamorphose,
coats of calcite adhere over the years,
are water-polished to pearls.

Christine Selwyn

We are eating juicy red peppers and white village bread. On the unfinished terrace with bare cement and a view of Rila. There is a spot of snow on the blue peaks. Rila seems so near, as if you could stretch your hand and touch it.

It's autumn. The kind of autumn where you get the right balance of freshness and warmth. Rustling leaves, mostly bright yellow. The trees shine with sunlit aureoles. There are no railings on the terrace, some vines have climbed up but are not clinging to anything.

In the evening, we will light up the stove in the bedroom behind the terrace, and we will toast thick slices of bread. We will eat at the big, wooden table, honey colour. We will spread yellow butter on the toasts, and it will melt. You will sprinkle dry savoury over the toasts. The middle part will soften slightly. Rila will become invisible from our curtainless bedroom.

From the table we will move to the wooden bed next to it. We will rest on the cotton mattress. You have thought of bringing washed sheets. We will strip off any unnecessary thoughts.

We will make love. You will want to record the sound of my breathing.

I will wake up when the sun shines in. Light; my feet and hands dropping their weight on the bed. You will be outside, working on the garden wall and repairing the gate. I will read my lectures to you, and you will wonder how I can persevere with such boring studies. The breeze will carry the smell of baked peppers and fire. Shall we go up the steep hill and reach that sunlit path above the forest?

We will imagine the possibility of living in this house. Is it too far to travel every day to Sofia and back?

In the winter, when we visit, we will use the little room on the first floor. You will show me the messy room opposite the derelict kitchen, and we will look at a pencil box from your grandparents' youth and wonder how objects were made to last then. We will sleep in the little room, where the stove is bigger, and the sofa extends into a bed. Not as honey-coloured as our sunlit summer bedroom. Grey stove, carpets – woven with petrol-green threads, subdued light.

I will finish my boring studies and apply for a new degree in France. I will ask you what will happen if I get a positive reply. You will say that I won't get it.

I will leave in September.

In April, you will suggest we get married. You will tell me that either we get married, or you will kiss the woman with the dark hair again. I will not say yes. I will take off the earrings you gave me, the silver sea urchins from Athens. I will let another man love me.

You will dream that I expect a baby. And it will be true. I will give birth without anaesthetic like you would have wished me to. I will dream that you have a daughter. And it will be true. Every year, I will write *All the best* in an email. We will not ask tricky questions. I will wake up and wonder where you've gone. So will you. We will try to build proper families. We will have salt-and-pepper hair. We will have neurosis and obsessive-compulsive disorder.

We will meet. We will tremble. We will be reasonable.

I will leave the man I've tried to love.

We will hope. We will see psychotherapists. We will get healthy. You will plant a thousand apple trees. I will write a thousand poems. Our children will learn to read and write and will surprise us with their talents and wisdom. We will learn that there are more important things than us. We will speak every now and then on the telephone and you will sigh. I will want to record your sigh.

I will wait for you and hope that you will come and fix the wooden furniture. You will not come. I will stop waiting. You will call to say that you are ready to leave, and you will ask me how we can make it. I will say that someone else made new furniture at home.

You will try to share your life with the mother of your children, then you will try to give up sharing your life with her. Try again. Have a second child. Give up.

We will agree to meet but neither of us will come to the *rendezvous*. I will stay with my furniture man, but every time before I come home, I will dream of you, and he will say that he understands. He will drive me to the airport, and I will imagine the house with the cement terrace and the sunlit trees. I will imagine that you and I will go there together and walk to that room with the grey stove. We will lie on the bed like children this time, together, pheeew – backwards, and hold hands. Your hand will be warm and rough. I don't know what it feels to hold my hand.

I will live happily with my modern family. You will find a modern way to live happily with yours. My husband will leave. The mother of your children will leave. We will speak on the phone again. You will be busy planting apples. I will be busy writing poems.

Ava Vasileva

The last of the day's sun dripped through the low-slung, identikit houses, as Dorothy Leonard raised her apple pie from the oven. There. The whole afternoon had spun by devoted solely to the pie, and on a Wednesday no less, when she had errands to run. Four round, dimpled and slightly mushed apples, windfalls from the Harpers next door, had gone into it. Plus, the last of the sugar and butter and Frank's favourite – condensed milk.

Frank! He'd be home soon. Wiping her hands on her apron, a curling black and white version of her husband stared back at her from the refrigerator, which was brand new, and a first for Sidney Street. "Nice as pie," she thought and went to apply her lipstick and await Frank's return.

"Get a load of this," said Frank. He closed the door, stamping his boots, and flopped a large folder crammed with papers onto Dorothy's carefully laid table.

"Frank ..." she protested but he, too excited by its contents to sit, simply crowed, "It's finished."

Dorothy's eyes closed. Behind her lids, she could see a map of wasted evenings. Frank, pipe in hand, booming out plans to leave behind the world of advertising and make it big. This was his latest.

Page after page of well-intentioned copy fanned out across the knives and plates. A corner of one, which simply read "Believe!" dangled into the slightly warm butter and dripped its way over Dorothy's checked tablecloth.

"The Seven Steps to Success!" began Frank. He gathered the papers into some semblance of order and placed himself in front of Dorothy. She, in turn, dabbed the drips of butter with her finger and considered whether to listen.

"Step One," he roared, "Articulate! To be successful," he went on, "one must articulate one's desires. What do you want to achieve?" he posed. Dorothy noticed a sprig of unannounced hair that had recently housed itself in Frank's left nostril. His skin had taken on an almost ruddy hue and veins peppered his nose. Should she answer?

"Being successful," continued Frank (no response needed), "requires that you articulate what you want from life. Have a clear plan and make it happen."

Dorothy thought mournfully about the apple pie, now cooling beyond its peak on the kitchen counter.

"Step Two: Ruminate!" He cleared his throat. "Think about how you're to put your plans into action. Skimp on this step," he warned no one in particular, "and you risk falling at the first hurdle."

"Step Three" continued Frank, "Abandon! Are your loved ones holding you back? Do your friends and family understand your drive for success?

If not, cut them out. Abandon anything – and anyone – that stands in your way."

The curled black and white photo winked from the refrigerator. 1941 Frank, 22 years old, had a loping, giraffe-like walk. His curls, thick and black, were smoothed away from Dorothy's gaze by a goop of wax which, sometimes, in hot weather, would plop onto his tie and from there, to her dress. Their wedding was a sultry, late-summer Minnesotan affair in a sea of corn fields and friends. She had been happy.

"Step Four," said 1954 Frank, snapping back into view.

"Wait," Dorothy said.

"No, dear. Not now," Frank rushed almost breathless with haste. "You gotta hear Step Four!"

Dorothy stood up. Her wooden chair, with its carefully buttoned maroon cushion, squealed across the lino. As she assessed the pie, Frank's voice burbled on. There he was, in the corner of her eye, all shirt sleeves and paper, waving out a series of imperative verbs.

She spooned the now cold pie into two bowls. She started to chew. She felt the four windfall apples wash into her mouth, glued her teeth into the sugar and butter and felt the whole lot lodge downwards into her stomach.

Bitter, then sweet. Bitter sweet. Bittersweet pie.

In the distance, a blurred shadow, Frank was talking. "Take action!" he pronounced, his face illuminated by the dying sun, "Don't waste time!"

Dorothy picked up the remaining pie. Now cold, it had begun to congeal to its dish and the apples swam soggily in Frank's condensed milk. She readied her arm. A large wodge of pie scooped itself onto the ladle in her hand. Raising it above her head, and closing her eyes, she flung the contents of the spoon at Frank.

There was a slop. Time, and Frank, both stopped. Pie dropped aimlessly down the lilac kitchen walls, pooling at Frank's feet. A large piece of apple crowned his now still head and pieces of crumb decorated his shoulders. Finally, the afternoon sun dipped below the window. Frank gathered his apple-sprayed papers.

He stared upwards.

"Take action ..." he continued to say. But Dorothy had gone.

Megan Owen

LEAVING YORK
(After Frank Ormsby)

I should have left you more often, York –
shrugged off the press of your walls
and the shops' hot breath
to head east to the herons and kingfishers
out on the wide flat ings;

shouldn't have rented that attic
with the old bat's furniture but held out
for mod cons and heating with friends
who cooked and got drunk, unwound
and sometimes wound up with each other;

should have bought wheels I could lift
up steps, to park in the hallway in everyone's way
and struck out when I liked for those skies,
or west past the rich kids' playgrounds
over Clifton Bridge to the unkempt real;

shouldn't have got up before dawn
on weekdays to run, before learning
to savour the frosted towpath's
year-round autumn smell, trusting
that if you walk far enough

downstream a bridge will appear
like a sunrise to tracks once unreachable,
the Ouse as ever in spate
but new flood defences
for now, at least, unbreached.

Julia Deakin

PARADISE

Of all colours, orange shows best through fog
which gathers most days in the bay in summer.
Warm air rising from the Central Valley
ushers cool air from the ocean shoreward
to condense and cloud the almost persimmon orange
towers of the bridge before investing the city.
Fog has a nickname here, you write, and an X account.
Every day asks a question. In a bag by the door
you stash kit you need to live out
the aftermath of an earthquake.
Locked on a roof, you talked yourself down
while the smell of smoke gusted off the hills.
Between one wildfire and the next, you learn what it is
to point your camera on the streets of a town
burned to the ground in an afternoon.

Every day its question. A gap in the hedge
sees me crouch to parse from snow
comings and goings of moorhen, muntjac and fox,
the farm pond still frozen over,
ice in the ditches sewn with grains of air.

Patrick Yarker

DEATH OF A MOUSE

Baby mouse,
a barely-there
crumb-harvester
orphaned and
effortful

lively
mouse-runs:
kitchen, dining room
breakfast's bread-speckle
a feast.

But it's a jungle
out there: shared landings
luring with murderous
'treats'

and sure enough
this morning
a tiny corpse
on the kitchen floor

lifeless legs
outstretched
as if its dot of a heart
decided mid-scuttle
to cease.

Left an empty space:
we are less
one breath.

Stephanie Conybeare

NIGHTFALL, CHANDIGARH

tonight on Himalaya Marg
there will be no stars
they will have withdrawn
leaving to the street lights
and the blue flames of paraffin stoves
the job of lightening the darkness –
all along one side of the road
the side where the shops are
they are gathered
rickshaw pullers
street food sellers
squatting on the pavement
to cook their evening meal
one of them is washing his clothes and feet
in a bucket of water
another hurls a stick at a stray dog
the dog runs
looking over his shoulder
barking in protest
though he knows he is beaten
there are more men than dogs
the dogs don't stand a chance –
when the men have finished licking their fingers
they will put out the blue flames
and lie down on their hard beds
the smell of paraffin will dissipate slowly
like an oil spill at sea
someone will turn off the lights
and the stars will come out

Neil Rathmell

THICC DADS WHO VAPE FOR CHRIST

are hanging in their yards and Jesus loves them

because his life-dad was pretty thicc
and good with his hands

but he lived in the days
before vaping and even smoking

so Jesus never got to hang
with his life-dad quite like this

and ask him about his daily flavour
and chill in this specific way while his dad blows rings

he loves the thicc dads too
because they remind him of his big dad

viz they know how to work
and they also know how to rest

but without that temper
that temper used to freak him out

when Jesus went down to harrow hell
and found it was a bigger job than he expected

he called in his thicc dads
they had this easy way with sinners

*hey what's the problem fella you seem stuck
why don't we try ... oh wow thanks thicc dad*

they gave Lucifer a box mod
and taught them about rebuildable coils

and when it was time for Jesus
to ascend to his big dad

they sent him up on clouds
of candyfloss and watermelon ice

and he took a kit back for his dad

so they could vape together

the thicc dads are hanging in their yards
neither toiling nor spinning

blesséd be the thicc dads
you chunky beautiful lilies

Adrian Salmon

Glossary:
thicc – full-figured, curvaceous
box mod – part of a vape that contains the battery and electronics
rebuildable coils – coils vaporise the e-liquid in a vape; advanced vapers
build their own ('rebuildables') rather than purchasing pre-built coils.

REVIEWS

As always, we received many more books for review than we can respond to – over twenty in this submission window. You are welcome to send the editor books for consideration but there is no guarantee we will be able to place a review, unfortunately, due to constraints of space. Please observe the same submission windows as for poetry and prose.

***The Butterfly House* by Kathryn Bevis**
Seren
ISBN 9781781727553 pp 70 £10.99

I wanted to start the reviews this time by honouring Kathryn Bevis, whose death in May 2024 was a sad loss to the poetry community. We send deepest commiserations to her family, and all those poets who she inspired and supported.

In an interview with the Forward Arts Foundation, Kathryn Bevis expressed her 'gratitude' to poetry as an art form. This generosity of spirit – in the face of a terminal cancer diagnosis – was a hallmark of her writing and wider work: she was also instrumental in facilitating other people's writing, through her establishment of the 'The Writing School' online platform, in Winchester.

Bevis' death, after a late diagnosis of end-stage cancer, was anticipated, but still left the poetry community bereft; her contribution to poetry was out of all proportion to the duration of her active period as a poet. She started writing in 2018, in her forties, after decades of reading, writing and teaching poetry, and this close engagement with the art and craft of poetry is manifest throughout her work. It was a delight to review her debut pamphlet, *Flamingo*, in DC 47, and some of the poems that were most striking in that context are included in this longer collection, which is simply divided into sections labelled 'After' and 'Before' (her cancer diagnosis). The collection begins with her Forward Prize Shortlisted poem, 'My body tells me she's filing for divorce.'

Those of us who have experienced divorce may struggle to recognise the compassion she extends to the injured parties in this breakdown, as she faces her separation from not her marriage, but all of her life. In 'My Cancer as a Ring-Tailed Lemur' the phrase that struck me this time was:

> '… But the lemur and I
> get on okay. I figure she has a right to be here too.
> She is, in some important sense, endeared too.'

Animals, their characteristics and behaviours, crop up frequently in her toolkit; I had the pleasure of sharing a Zoom launch with Bevis for the Candlesticks *Wonky Animals* Pamphlet. Whether exotic or mundane, animals are metaphors for a life lived all the more intensely in the face of its imminent ending; a life in which nothing has to be perfect to be beautiful and be loved. She name-checks family members (her Nan-Nan, her husband Ollie, among others) who are especially loved, but Bevis knows that animals grieve, too. They also rage. The sequence of poems 'Translations of Grief' takes us through some of the stages identified by Kübler Ross – Denial, Anger and so on; here,

' … Zipped
in a zebra suit, my nostrils flare.

…I launch the designer handbag
Of myself, thrash my rail and mane, hoof
The box of tissues …

…My kick
Has force enough to break a crocodile's jaw.'

Alongside fauna, flora provide memorable images; 'Anagrams of Happiness' include

'… the winking silk of a spider's web'

And

'that fiddlehead of the fern's curled spine.'

In her imagining of her funeral ('Everyone will be there'), she is

'wearing a wicker dress.
Friends and relatives will braid in my bodice
a meadow, bright-tipped with the names
of their love: angelica, bluebell, cotton grass'.

In an interview with Poetry School, she explains how though she respects others' way of handling the issue, she chooses not to use the language of combat so often associated with a terminal diagnoses. We are enriched by this tactic, not least when we read

'every poem I write these days becomes
a love poem …

the way the name of each person
I love is part of a map that traces
the contours of my belonging,
each name the answer to a question
I didn't know how to ask.'

Poignant, powerful, brave, and beautiful, these poems cry out to be read and shared; in them, you will find answers to questions you did not know you had.

Hannah Stone

Leaving the Hills by **Tony Curtis**
Seren
ISBN 9781781727423   £10.99

This is the eleventh collection – and another excellent Seren production – from the multi-award winning Welsh poet and academic, Tony Curtis. Given his age – he was born in 1946 and made his print debut in 1974 – there is a sense of retrospective, of reviewing both a past and a present of very wide interests and sources in this collection. Which of us, indeed,

'…in a dark glass'

'Has not seen time's servant staring
Eyes closed into his death mask?' ('A Rebours/Spectre Flush')

At first glance the title and opening poem, 'Leaving the Hills,' might suggest a certain wistfulness, even a dose of 'hiraeth.' There is, maybe, some truth in this though the hills are not of Curtis's Welsh homeland but of Hollywood. The poem focuses on Aldous Huxley and his wife fleeing the 1961 wildfires that destroyed their home and treasured possessions and in the poem Huxley contemplates what is lost to the flames. In a real sense this is what this collection does – allowing Curtis to sift through his work and life since his last collection of several years ago and memorialise what might otherwise have been lost. Huxley doesn't seem bothered:

'I felt
Extraordinarily clean, extraordinarily clear
Given more time,
That could have been a fresh start.'

One suspects too that Curtis may well have the same perspective. He has suggested that this collection might be his last though equally this 'clearing of the decks' may hopefully presage a similar 'fresh start.'

The collection ranges widely across subject matters; ekphrastic poems, poems rooted in history, a neat sequence about the boxer Jimmy Wilde, buried in my hometown, a jazz suite and a powerful and moving sequence on the fiftieth anniversary of the Aberfan tragedy complemented by stunning contemporary photographs. This approach has its advantages and disadvantages. The scope of the poetry is to be applauded in its demonstration of the poet's ability to create meaning out of many stimuli and, through his craft, to place the reader firmly in a context, a situation. Occasionally though this approach can result in poems that require a lot of narrative, a lot of telling and which, in the end, leave the reader informed but not necessarily enlivened. Where they work – as in 'Climbing the Overhang' where a church has been re-purposed as a climbing centre – they dazzle with a deft feel for the telling image and the startling juxtapositions.

There are many poems inspired by artists and paintings. Ekphrastic poems can be hit and miss – if they do not add anything to what is essentially a description of the artwork then they are tepid. They must reveal what Robin Reid Drake called "the hidden truths" that emerge from the poet's experience of the work. Curtis can do just this though the standout poem focuses on a photograph – thus 'Claude and Chouchou at Le Moulleau, 1916', with the photograph of Debussy and his daughter on the page, works well in demonstrating how a moment fixed in a still image can carry past, present and future in itself. The close:

> 'their dog has heard something in the pines
> and turns his head to look away'

communicates perfectly the sense the poet must have that there is always something happening out of the picture that a poem must recognise and deal with.

This a fine, varied and interesting collection. At his best, Curtis manages, as he puts it in his poem dedicated to Peter Prendergast, the Welsh landscape painter,

> 'to guide the pencil and charcoal
> Impression
>
> marks of our being here
> the journey.' ('The Nant Ffrancon Valley').

There is no pomposity here. 'Further Instructions,' one of the closing poems, riffs on the scattering of his ashes and locates them where the living poet has also located himself, in a loved pastoral Gower land/seascape where the best that can be hoped for is that some golfer waiting to play might catch the act of scattering:

> 'see the smudge of a boat out fishing
> and that will quicken the heart.'

There is a strong sense of acceptance in the poems that all things go on as they should; there is sadness in life but Curtis is also aware that there is also joy. A collection to dip into again and again.

Patrick Lodge

Some Indefinable Cord by **Katy Mahon**
Dreich Slims
ISBN 9781873412558 pp26 £5.00

It is always good to see the output of the many small indie poetry publishers, and Scottish based Dreich (currently 'resting') has produced some very good looking volumes, with attractive front and end pages and well laid out text (not always the case with poetry pamphlets).This pocket-sized gem gives Mahon the opportunity to commemorate the life of her poet father, Derek, to whom this volume of 25 poems is dedicated. It also celebrates the craft of being alive, in all its rich dimensions.

Mahon is a musician as well as writer, and this is communicated not only through imagery, but in the way lines are held, weighed, and released, and the careful attention to the sound of the poems. 'The Irish Goodbye' has lines that recall the way an oenophile will hold a mouthful of wine, and swill it around for the depths of flavour, before going for the aftertaste:

'The clock hits its furious beat click click
against the oven, the plinth, and the mind kickstarts
the whole event
again.'

The pattern of repeated vowel sounds and the insistent rhythm speaks to me of a musician's ear (as well as the connoisseur's palate!).

The intensity of sounds is also expressed through touches of synaesthesia, in 'Music at night reflects':

'Semiquavers float to the door
with salty voices ...

... I yearned for a calling,
felt the raging purple aroma
of an unforgiving Chopin *glissando*.'

There is a strong sense of the elegiac in these poems: even at their brightest, they speak of the sense that it is because life is ephemeral that it is to be treasured.

Whilst these poems clearly grow from personal experience, local to the author and her father, they also give glimpses into a wider world; we experience a Shamanic drum and a Goan blanket ('Mourning Time'). 'Stauros' uses the image of

'That Greek cross you wore,
    shining squat against your skin'

as both an icon of remembrance and

' ... a tool resting before
hammering something
into oblivion.'

In lines like these, Mahon shows her skill in moving from a close-up focus on the concrete to something broader, inviting the reader to share in the experience of

'the dull light of English winter' and the surprising

' … past kindness
    so often automatically rejected.'

A series of thoughtful vignettes, these poems draw you in with a quiet insistence.

Hannah Stone

A Coalition of Cheetahs by Doreen Gurrey
Smith|Doorstop Books, the Poetry Business
ISBN 978 -1- 914914 -72-0   £6.00

Doreen Gurry won the Poetry Business International book and Pamphlet Prize with this excellent collection.

Her poems often draw on the past without sentimentality, evoking a sense of place or period through visual or physical details. Such imagery enables the expression of intense but controlled emotion. The first poem 'Post-war Settlement' sets the tone, starting with the memory of a stained-glass panel in a door, to move onto a quiet study in suppressed grief and loss:

'Sometimes she has to shut the shop early, tiptoe upstairs
to lie quietly under clean white sheets.'

The same technique is seen in 'Cologne' which develops from a memory of an exotic bottle of 4711 Cologne perfume in her grandmother's handbag, to a profound statement about modern life: 'the bottle was plastic'.

There is an emphasis on female voices throughout. Recognizable family situations are opened out to reveal the harshness of women's lives, past and present. In 'Exile', a beach scene leads us to the emigrant women who dared to risk a sea journey to escape their poverty in the United Kingdom: 'all the ache and grind that pulled them down as surely as drowning.'

Gurrey frequently uses small details to convey a great deal about character, as in 'Timepiece'. There, she contrasts her grandfather's and her grandmother's mirrors. His 'hung by a single gold chain/set between china dogs with sooty noses who guarded his baccy box.' Hers was 'an altogether smaller affair, set between two stiff brushes.'

A wide range of themes and situations are developed in this small collection. Two interesting poems draw on illustrations in the 13th century bestiary at Holy Trinity, York (the wolf and bear). Gwen John's relationship with Rodin inspires another two poems: 'Letter to Rodin' and 'I have hurried dreadfully …' Literary sources are a further source of inspiration. Ophelia's song in *Hamlet* is recreated in the lyrical 'There's rue for you; and here's some for me,' while in 'Great Expectations' Gurrey moves from rereading a novel to grief for her dead mother. There is some dry humour, as in 'Vocab.' which plays with collective nouns (the title is an example of these) and 'Blown' which recalls a childhood romance. Whatever the subject, the verse form is tightly controlled and the tone quiet, but often suggestive of deep emotion.

If I have a criticism, it is that *A Coalition of Cheetahs* is a bit too much of a mixed bag. Poems about the river goddess Usa ('Ouse'), cave paintings ('La Pasiega, Spain') a visitor ('Guest') and student days ('Rule Britannia') sit uneasily beside recreations of historical suffering, or intense personal loss. A bigger collection would have done the poet more justice and enabled the development of her themes, but this was a competition entry constrained by pamphlet length. All the poems are the work of an experienced writer in control of her medium, and clearly a worthy winner of the Poetry Business competition.

Pauline Kirk

Scottish Religious Poetry from the Sixth Century to the present **edited by Linden Bicket, Emma Dymock and Alison Jack**
Saint Andrew Press
ISBN 9780800830479 pp 316 £25

This weighty tome, described as 'a comprehensive collection of poetry from Scotland in English, Gaelic and Scots' provided some insights into the religious life, cultural identity and psyche of the Scots, whether the poems were overtly religious or not (the vast majority were). A scholarly introduction sets the scene and defends the decisions made about what was included, and editorial decisions such as to 'remove the original version of a translated poem when it was not written in a living language.' This allowed space for a wider range of poets to be included, including some millennial writers (the poems are published in chronological order, with (where known) dates for the poets). Clearly editorial discussions had taken place about how to define the concept of 'Scottish': George Gordon (more commonly known perhaps as Byron) gets included, on the basis of having been educated in his mother's city of Aberdeen (though he was born in London, and subsequent education took place at Harrow and Cambridge). Similarly Imtiaz Dharker is allocated a space not on the grounds of birth but where she was educated, and her self-identification as a 'Scottish Muslim Calvinist.' These editorial choices promoted reflection on broader issues than the quality of the poetry included: reading this volume, you could not avoid issues of identity, history, and cultural tensions, including relationships to south of the border. Meticulous detail is paid to indices, biographies and other academic paraphernalia. I was glad to meet some familiar and new voices here – though was sorry not to see my favourite Scottish poet, Niall Campbell, included in the selection. Makers for Scotland Lochhead, Kay and Jamie are represented.

The poems include Biblical renditions, hymnography, poems of dissent, poems expressive of Scottish identity. In a short review it is not possible to go into much detail, but some random aspects that struck me included how late into the modern period the Devil is personified, as in Violet Jacob's 'The Deil'; satire (particularly political, such as Somhairle MacGill-Eain's 'Scotus Erigena'); and a rare example of ecumenism in Ruaraidh MacThòmais' 'Playing Football with a Prophet'. Nan Shepherd's sonnet 'Real Presence' exemplifies how the landscape can be as much a source of veneration as any dogmatic divine presence: I loved her description of

'... Venus, when her white unearthly glow
Sharpens like awe of skies as green as ice.'

I can't speak for the production values of the book as I was sent an unwieldy unbound A4 copy, but in its finished form I recommend this as a welcome text to dip into for refreshment, inspiration, and a strong sense of shared identity.

Hannah Stone

Spin **by Laurie Bolger**
Smith|Doorstop Books, the Poetry Business
ISBN 978-1-914914-70-6 £6.00

The Poetry Business has done sterling work for years, promoting new and little-known poets. *Spin* is one of a series of pamphlets they have published recently giving new writers exposure. It is very different to *A Coalition of Cheetahs*.

The title conveys its mood: a breathless headlong spin through all aspects of a life lived at full pace, both good and bad. It feels as if the poet is writing under stress, feeling the pressure of modern life and of being a woman struggling on the edge. Poems like 'Birds' and 'Boxercise' convey a deep, barely suppressed anger:

'imagine you're ducking
under a washing line

I've done that my whole life' (*'Boxercise'*)

The verse forms are in keeping: experimentally set out stanzas, rapid rhythms, short lines, disjointed expressions, gaps within lines to create pauses. Poems often start with a vivid glimpse of a scene or image and then move on to another idea it has generated. Sometimes the connections shade into absurdity or surrealism, as in 'After Class' and 'Yoga'. Even then, they are grounded in the details of an ordinary woman's life. Occasionally the breathless pace feels rather forced. The lines in 'Boxes' are so short that they are arranged together like a prose poem, with hatching to denote endings. Bolger's experiments can work well however, notably in 'SILVO', where the pauses highlight the endless negative instructions given to young girls.

Settings vary from keep fit classes, to restaurants and working men's clubs and pubs, or memories of being a little girl. The focus is on character, or the lived (or imagined) experiences of the poet. The long prose poem 'Roadside Café' is a good example. It starts in a real situation, full of atmospheric detail, but becomes increasingly surreal as it traces the breakdown of a relationship. 'Washing' takes a mundane situation – watching a washing machine – to lead us into childhood memories of the poet's street and the women who lived on it. The final lines are a touching tribute to the way they cared for their men 'until the end'. In 'Stars' Bolger conveys the deterioration of a woman near to breakdown. 'Scenes Involving a Kitchen Table' develops its mundane setting to encompass a whole life.

Some poems like 'Eton Mess' or 'Spin Bike 53' are bitter. They, too, are sharply and truthfully observed. I particularly liked 'Mary and John's Ruby wedding, the Working Men's Club' and 'Looking at Mum,' with its stinging last stanza summarizing her mother's advice for life:

'stay away from the deserts and sweets
push your boobs up like two jellies'

Laurie Bolger is a new and distinctive voice. It will be interesting to see what she goes on to write.

Pauline Kirk

A Darker Way by Grahame Davies
Seren
ISBN 978178172714 £10.99

If the title might suggest to a casual reader a descent into a Goth vision of the world, there will be disappointment – though the poet confesses to being once 'a teenage goth.' It is, however, a revealing title as Davies, the much-honoured bi-lingual Welsh poet, academic, librettist, novelist, psycho-geographer and the Church in Wales's first Director of Mission and Strategy here explores issues of faith, spirituality and poetry with no lapse into mere sentimentality, just a hard-headed enquiring born of experience and grounded philosophy. Now in his 60s, Davies is certainly permitted to adopt a more reflective perspective. The second poem in the collection, archly entitled 'Farewell to Poetry,' might seem to suggest a waning of the muse – poems

> '…used to stack up,
> waiting in the sky…'

– but the evidence of this collection belies that worry.

Davies recognises that writing poetry is not easy – the poet almost as anguished martyr compelled to write – describing it as

> '…an open wound.
> I treasured it, stigmatic
> without sainthood,
> weeping words, the grief
> a price worth paying.' ('Scar')

The writing of poetry was a travail – 'Peace makes no poetry' ('Scar') – not least because of the poet's desire

> '…to go deeper, darker, inward all the time'

looking for

> '…some secret, maybe hidden in the night.'('Solstice').

Here is a poet of integrity laying bare that which drove him to write. Well he might

> '…walk on…a darker way' ('Centenary Square, Birmingham')

but there is a cost here. Carol Rumens has described Davies as 'a contemporary Philip Larkin' and there is, indeed, that poet's 'sense of melancholy isolation' here. The older, contemplative Davies might recognise this but now is content to abjure the treadmill – 'the need to make poetry' – and simply enjoy

> 'Silence after sound,
> and solitude after society.' ('Farewell to Poetry')

In this collection the reader may enjoy the fruits of this more laid-back approach. Davies makes a kind of poetry out of the chance, slight encounters, the unpromising exchanges of humans. Here are sentiments simply expressed but powerfully felt; there is a lyrical content pervading many of these poems. Away from Wales, in Brooklyn on a wet, November night, Davies can see the positives as each departing jet out of JFK might emphasise that you are unequivocally *here,* but

> '…every season teaches us to choose
> rain where we love, not sunshine far away.'('Rain in Brooklyn').

Like others, Davies faces the fiftieth anniversary of the Aberfan disaster – he was actually a cub journalist at the time and the first one on the scene – and offers a most moving sequence full of humility at the impossibility of comprehending or retelling. His emotion is clear but never sentimental; he is right to say simply that

'The hearts of every woman, every man,
go to the rows of graves at Aberfan.' ('The Graves at Aberfan').

These poems are suffused in almost a non-denominational spirituality. Davies might write that

'I know my faith has failed from year to year,
and my heart has lost the hope it used to hold' ('Adre' Dros Dolig')

but there are compensations aplenty, not least in the honest search, the being in the world. There may be fewer answers but

'You know, at least,
you have not hidden from the questions'('Between the Stormclouds and the Sea').

Rejecting the promises of an easy teleology, Davies recognises that each day actually

'is a pilgrimage to poverty,
life leaves you one day poorer every night' ('Questions')

but an easy pastoralism may compensate as God's

'…wisdom is the sunlight and the snow.
(His) beauty in the rosebud and the briar.' ('Sacred Fire').

This is a substantial, enjoyable collection; crafted poems heavy with thought, uncertainty and searching but joyous in their music and affirmation. As Yeats put it in 'After Long Silence', despite all
'…we descant, and yet again descant.' Davies would heartily agree:

'But we still sing, because the night's so lonely
We still sing, for every birth is a beginning,
and hope is in a mother's arms again.'('Adre' Dros 'Dolig')

Patrick Lodge

The Remaining Men **by Martin Figura**
Cinnamon Press
ISBN 9781788641548 pp79 £9.99

An observation made by several reviewers praising Figura's latest collection is that it is 'unsentimental,' which perhaps begs the question why this is so refreshing? As a poet and reviewer, I'd say that where the personal emotions of the writer are subsumed to a more inclusive emotional space, there is room for *every* reader to 'find' themselves in the words and places. Sometimes poets who indulge in a very individualistic emotional splurge can alienate or exclude readers who don't share their perspective or identity. Plenty of the poems in this collection *are* deeply personal, and reveal elements of his own biography, but this does not dominate. Rather, it suggests that Figura himself, through childhood trauma, has grown into an identity as a man who 'remains' very much present, despite being 'the wrong sort of clever' ('Liar'). Figura's focus in this collection is on the eponymous 'remaining' men, but this does not at all mean that this is not a collection to be enjoyed by women. And whether or not you had an existing interest in past British Prime Ministers, traumatised soldiers, or redundant miners, this collection engages, stimulates and challenges its reader.

A handful of pictures are included in the volume, their titles listed in the contents in exactly the same way as the poems, a nice touch; the

' ... tongueless pit boot fossilised
in crazed mud' ('Seams')

is especially striking, reminding us that when you are a survivor

' ... Some will do okay, others thrive
and some of you will drown.'

The cover image also combines that sense of the personal with the more universal; the bottom half of a face; a thin-lipped mouth, wrinkles suggesting resilience and humour above a meticulously sharply knotted paisley tie, and a fawn cardigan. Many of us will have recognise this wardrobe choice, but omitting the eyes of the man creates a sense of discretion, privacy almost.

The title poem is at the heart of the collection, and evokes for me a sense of the Antony Gormley's 'Another Place' sculpture (one hundred cast iron figures facing the sea at Crosby Beach, Merseyside, not far from the

'frontier town that takes its name from mucky water drained
from nearby land' ('Looked After Children, Blackpool').

The eponymous men

' ... just stood there, looking out over the scarred coast
through red-rimmed eyes to the rough brown sea ...

When children asked what they were, not everyone
Could remember and of those that did, few were believed.'

The detailed acknowledgments are testament to Figura's collaborative skill, and range of reference – poems commissioned by The Soldiers' Charity, Salisbury NHS, and Adult Social Care services in Norfolk among others.

Despite the serious subject matter of many of the poems there is humour, warmth and a generous sensitivity. For me, the long multi-part prose poem 'Carers' sums up the achievement of the collection:

'Jeopardy fell heaviest for those with the least and you were among them; forgive us for this. Poems weigh no more, maybe less than applause. I wish I had more; I wish words were a feast.'

Rest assured, Martin, your words have fed and nourished us.

Hannah Stone

STRIKE by Sarah Wimbush
Stairwell Books
ISBN 978-1-913432-80-5 pp 86 pages £15

Not just a book of poems: a work of art. And not just a work of art but a document, a corrective, a fist raised in defiance of the accepted story of what happened 40 years ago, in parts of this dis-United Kingdom.

The first poem, *Our Language*, opens with the words 'This is the voice.' Finally, we are to hear from the miners, those men, those fathers, uncles and cousins: that scarred, fractured, sweat-stained, lung-damaged band of brothers with the ingrained dust tattoos they can't wash from their skin, their backs stooping under the weight of their fathers' fathers. We hear from the kids, those hungry threadbare kids, robbed of a future, scrabbling for slack. From the filleted, broken, boarded-up communities. And we hear from the women: those wonderful, resourceful, pragmatic, indefatigable women feeding, marching, patching back together that which Thatcher tore asunder, every day.

The photographs are from 1984/5 and some have been 'paired' with poems written many years later, while in other cases the poems were clearly written *to* the photos: 'STOP,' 'Picketing at Penrhiwceiber,' 'BASTARD NACODS SCABS' and 'Women Against Pit Closures' (her lips, the curve of a pickaxe) to name a few. The most moving of these is the crowded room shown in Keith Pattison's picture *Men receiving hardship money at Easington Colliery, County Durham*, which has the pathos and beauty of a Caravaggio and is accompanied by the fine, sparse poem 'Miners Leaning Forwards':

'Mortal. Men cropped and cast
into grey corners.

Men as sticks, men as shadow.

Men's pockets lined with bits of string.
Seams. Grit.

... They gather around hardship money
Like new fathers.'

One photographer even gets his own poem, 'Picture Man':

' ...and John Harris forever eats carrots,
mash and gravy in Kersley pit canteen.'

Each couplet from the eight that make up the poem 'Women's Support Groups', contains the refrain 'they stand', until in the final one the women

'pull their daughters forward and stand them in the light.'

A poem that tells you all you need to know about solidarity and the integral role of women in this struggle and in their communities. All of which is key to the re-balancing effect of this collection: this strike was not just about the men and their jobs – it was never about the money – it was about the lives and the families built around that work.

Wimbush is clear who the real 'enemies within' were: the obvious, Thatcher is named, with 'her bloody woman's hands', as is McGregor, and

'Maggie's Judas
David Hart' –

a man described by the Daily Telegraph as 'Thatcher's unsung hero who broke the miners' strike.' Then there are the scabs, the Police and the BBC with its 'misreporting:'

'Lies. Lies and more bollocks.'

She is also clear about consequences: 'Coal Kid' is a poem twinned with a photo of a grubby, skinny kid, all knock-knees in a too-big jumper coming back with a wrap of chips. The poem is a series of 14 questions:

'When did the sole begin to come away on your shoe?

... Have you ever had a dream?'

At the book's launch, the poem 'Queen Coal' was so well-received, Wimbush was obliged to read it again. It is not hard to understand why; it is a powerhouse of a poem that should ricochet off classroom walls as it is taught on the National Curriculum.

'These are the women...these are the women...these monarchs
Coal Queens. Pit-brow lasses. Lionesses.'

I grew up in West Yorkshire, a mining area and was seventeen at the time of the strike. I went to football matches where fans of southern teams would wave mocking bank notes while singing about poverty, Thatcher, and having a job. The anger this book brings back to the surface is very real. But the book is not just about anger, it is also filled with grief for what has been taken; not lost, but taken.

Above all, this book is about the importance of remembering the truth of events, to be forever reminded how far the state, and the powerful will go to keep the hands of the people away from the levers of power, in this democracy.

This book is timely. It is, at long last, *the voice* of those deliberately shattered communities. It is, to my mind, the most important book of poetry published this year.

Nick Allen

INDEX OF AUTHORS

THANK YOU

Dream Catcher and Stairwell Books would like to extend a big thank you to everyone who has contributed to Dream Catcher over the last 19 years. In that time Dream Catcher has grown from its humble start as a student project into a major international literary journal. The list of contributors over the years below is not exhaustive but wherever you are, whoever you are, if you have contributed to the success of Dream Catcher in any way, as artist, designer, publisher, contributor, printer, subscriber or financier: thank you very much.

AA Marcoff, Abegail Morley, Adam Price, Adam Strickson, Adele Karmazyn, Adrian Blackledge, Adrian Buckner, Adrian Markle, Adrian Salmon, Adrian Spendlow, Adrian Tellwright, Adrienne Silcock, Afifa Emutallah, Agnes Read, Ahren Warner, Aiden O'Reilly, Alan Dent, Alan Dunnett, Alan Dyson, Alan Gillott, Alan Glasby, Alan Smith, Albert Herranz, Alessio Zanelli , Alex Hales, Alex Josephy, Alex Rourke, Alex Shearer, Alex Smith, Alex Toms, Alexander Williamson, Alexis Lykiard, Ali Pardoe, Alice Harrison, Alice Tomlinson, Alice Walker, Alice West, Alice Wooledge Salmon, Alicia Fernández, Alison Brackenbury, Alison Milner, Alison Mordey, Alistair Heys, Alistair Paterson, Alix Willard, Allessio Zanelli, Alwyn Gornall, Amari Hamadene , Amina Alyal, Amy Lane, Ana Vidosavljevc, and Patricia Prime, Andre Mangeot, Andrea Bowd, Andrea Michael, Andrea Small, Andrew Darlington, Andrew Detheridge, Andrew Greary, Andrew Hanson, Andrew Mayne, Andrew Nightingale, Andrew Oldham, Andria Cooke, Andria Jane Cooke, Andy Armitage, Andy Fletcher, Andy Humphrey, Andy J. Campbell, Angela Arnold, Angela Cooke, Angela France, Angela Howarth Martinot, Angela Morkos, Angela Readman, Angela Rigsby, Angelica Krikler, Anita Ngai, Ann Gibson, Ann Heath, Anna Akhmatova, Annamarie Austin, Anne Caldwell, Anne Eyries, Anne Rees, Anne Ryland, Anne Symons, Annemarie Cooper, Annie Clarkson, Annie Edge, Annie Kedzlie, Anthony Costello, Anthony Head, Anthony Suter, Antony Dunn, Arthur Arnold, Ashleigh R. Davies, Ashleigh Watson, Audrey Greaves, Ava Patel, Ava Vasileva, Avril Joy, Ayelet McKenzie, Aziz Dixon, Barbara Cumbers, Barbara Dordi, Barbara Ponomareff, Barry Dempster , Barry Tebb, Becca Miles, Becci Louise, Bel Wallace, Belinda Cooke, Belinda Rimmer, Beliz McKenzie, Ben Benison, Ben Macnair, Ben Wilkinson, Bernadette Rule, Bill Dodd, Bill Fitzsimons, Bob Beagrie, Bob Cooper, Brenda Williams, Brian Docherty, Brian Maycock, Brian McCusker, Briar Wood, Bridget Thomasin, Bruach Kandinsky Mhor, Bruce Adkins , Bruce McRae, C M Buckland, C. L. Spillard, C. M. Buckland, C.P. Stewart, Caitlin Brown, Caleb Armstrong, Callum Beesley, Carmella de Keyser, Carmina Masoliver, Carol Butler, Carol Coiffait, Carol Farrelly, Carol Topolski, Carole Bromley, Carole Coates, Carole Coffait, Carole Dalton, Carole Houlston, Carole Thirlaway, Caroline Burton, Caroline de Verteuil, Caroline Walling, Carolyn Oulton, Cath Heinemeyer, Catherine Heinemayer, Catherine Jenkins, Catherine Mair, Catherine Smith, Cathy Grindrod, Cathy Whittaker, Cedric Pickin, Ceinwen E Cariad Haydon, Ceinwen Haydon, Celia Baines, Char March, Charles Bennett, Charles Douglas, Charles Tomson, Charlotte McCormac, Charlotte Oliver, Charlotte Silveston, Charlotte Wetton, Chris Bousfield, Chris Deakins, Chris Firth, Chris Hardy, Chris Jones, Chris Kinsey, Chris McCabe, Chris Pannell, Chris Preddle, Chris Rice, Chris Rivers, Chris Scriven, Chris Tutton, Christian McCulloch, Christian Ward, Christine McNeill, Christine Selwyn, Christopher M James, Christopher Twose, Ciaran Buckley, Ciáran Dermott, Claire Booker, Claire Kotecki, Clare Crossman, Clare McKay, Clare Pollard, Clare Wigzell, Clifford Liles, Clint Wastling, Clive Donovan, Clive Eastwood, Colette Coen, Colette Longbottom, Colin Hopkirk, Colin Pink, Colin Speakman, Connie Bott, Corbett Buchly, Craig Kurtz, Crysse Morrison, D M Street, D.M. de Silva, D.V.Cooke, Daithidh MacEochaidh, Dalton Harrison, Damon Young, Dan Stathers, Dan Vevers, Dan Wyke, Dane Cobain, Daniel Abdal Hayy Moore , Daniel Gustafsson, Daniel Nemo, Daniel Richardson, Daniel Shooter, Daniel Skyle, Daniel Souza, Dannie Abse, Daphne Rock, Darryl Donaghue, Dave Hubble, Dave Mason, Dave Medd, Dave Pescod, Dave Wynne-Jones, David Atkinson, David Batten, David Baumforth, David Burridge, David Constantine, David Cooke, David Crann, David Danbury, David Ford, David Gill, David Greenslade , David Grubb, David Hale, David Hamson, David Harmer, David Haskins, David Hillen, David J Costello, David Lewitzky, David Lightfoot, David Lukens, David McVey, David O'Hanlon, David Olsen, David Sapp, David Sim, David Susswein, David Thompson, David Trame , David Troupes, David Winner, Debi Knight, Debjani Chatterjee, Deborah Harvey, Deborah Maudlin, Dee Rimbaud, Delilah Heaton, Denise Bennett, Denise McSheehy, Derek Collins, Derek Crook, Derek Smith, Dharmavadana, Diana Cant, Diana Powell, Diana Sanders, Diana Webb, Diane Cadman, Dick Ockleton, Dick Smith, Dike-ogu Chukwumerije , Divya Mathur, DM Street, Dmitry Blizniuk, Dominic Rivron, Don Rhodes, Donna Langevin , Donna Pucciani , Donna Williams, Doreen Hinchliffe, Douglas Thompson, Dylan James Harper, Eaban Ni Shuilebhain, Ece Sakar , Echo, Ed Limb, Ed Reiss, Edward Alport, Edward Storey, Edwin Stockdale, Eileen Neil, Elaine Baker, Elaine Ewart, Elaine Thomas CBE, Eleanor Higginson, Eleanor Porter, Elisabeth Jeffreys, Elisabeth Kelly, Eliza Dear, Eliza Mood, Elizabeth Barrett, Elizabeth Hare, Elizabeth Smither , Elizabeth Stott, Ellen Boucher, Ellen Plant, Emily Drew, Emily Zobel Marshall, Emma Lee, Emma Timpany, Emma Whitehall, Emma-Jane Arkady, Emmaline O'Dowd, Estill Pollock, Eva Ghoshal, Eva Strittmatter, Eve Chancellor, Eve Kalyva, F J Williams, F. Mary Callan, F.J. Williams, Fiona Shillito, Fiona Theokritoff, Fionola Scott, Florian Rose, Fokkina McDonnell, Frances Thimann, Frank Brindle, Fred Johnston, Fred Schofield, Fred Voss, Freya Horsley, Gabrielle Van Amburg, Gaia Holmes, Gail Denby, Gareth Adams, Gareth Culshaw, Gareth Spark, Gary Allen , Gary Gottfriedson , Gary Jude, Gavin Boyter, Gay McKenna, Gene Groves, Genny Rahtz, Geoff Stevens, Geoffrey Loe, George Jowett, Gerald Green, Gerald Kells, Gerald Killingworth, Geraldine Bell, Gerard Benson, Gerry Stewart, Gill Horitz, Gill McEvoy, Gillian Drake, Gillian Ewing, Ginna Wilkerson, Glen Proctor, Gloria Grove-Stephensen, Glyn Hughes, Gordon Scapens, Gordon Wardman, Gordon Wilson, Grahaeme Barrasford Young, Graham Brodie, Graham Buchan, Graham Dawson, Graham High, Graham Hubbard, Graham Mort, Grant Tabard, Greg Forshaw, Greg McGee, Greg Smith, Gregor M Lapka, Gregory Gilbert Grumbs , Gregory Heath, Greta Ross, Guy Jones, Gwen Sayers, H. Alder, Hadi Panahi, Hannah Faoileán, Hannah Stone,

Harry Hendrick, Harry Malkin, Harry Slater, Heather Deckner, Heather Hughes, Heather Murphy, Heather Stack, Helen Burke, Helen Cox, Helen Entwisle, Helen Goodway, Helen Heery, Helen Kampfner, Helen Kay, Helen Mort, Helen Parker, Helen Pinoff, Helen Shay, Hélène Demetriades, Henry Marsh, Hilaire, Hilary Hares, Hilary Robinson, Hoffman Aipira, Holly Sykes, Howard Benn, Howard Jeeves, Hubert Moore, Iain Blair-Brown, Iain Twiddy, Ian Brook, Ian Caws, Ian Chapman, Ian Clarke, Ian Duhig, Ian Emberson, Ian Harrow, Ian McCulloch, Ian McMillan, Ian Parks, Ian Seed, Ian Stuart, Idris Caffrey, Ilse Pedler, Imogen Godwin, India Russell, Ingeborg Bachmann, Isabel Greenslade, Isobel Dixon, Ivan McGuinness, J Burke, J.Twm, Jac Shortland, Jack Debney, Jack Tindle, Jackie Kay, Jacqueline P Haskell, Jacqueline Sousa, Jacqueline Zacharias, Jade Smith, Jagoda Olender, Jaimes Lewis Moran, James B Nicola, James Christie, James Costello O'Reilly, James Dheal, James Fountain, James Fountain, James Manlow, James McGarth, James Miller, James Norcliffe, James Richards, Jamie Lynch, Jamie Osborn, Jan Conn, Jan FitzGerald, Jan Stacey, Jane Ayrie, Jane Poulton, Jane Sharp, Jane Stuart, Janet Hancock, Janet Harper, Janet Laugharne, Jason Monios, Jaspreet Mander, Javier Bergia, Jay Merill, Jean Harrison, Jean Stevens, Jeff Phelps, Jeffrey Joseph, Jekwu Anyaegbuna, Jennie Christian, Jennie E Owen, Jennifer A Miller, Jennifer Compton, Jennifer Copley, Jennifer Footman, Jenny Brice/Argante, Jenny Clarkson, Jenny Hamlett, Jenny Hockey, Jenny Johnson, Jenny McRobert, Jenny Owens, Jenny Robb, Jenny Stephen, Jenny Swann, Jeremy Duffield, Jeremy Page, Jeremy Platt, Jeremy Punter, Jeremy Worman, Jess Richard, Jessica Lim, Jim Greenhalf, Jim Sinclair, Jimmy Rodda, Jo Brandon, Jo Haley, Jo Haslam, Jo Heather, Jo Hemmant, Jo Pearson, Joan Byrne, Joan Johnston, João Sousa, Jocelyne Thébault, Joe Kane, Joe Spivey, Joe Warner, Joe Williams, Joel Lane, John Andrew, John Ashley, John Christopher Johnson, John Coopey, John Davies, John Dolan, John F Buckley, John Fewings, John Gilham, John Gosnell, John Greeves, John Greeves, John Hyde, John Irving Clarke, John Kidd, John Lindley, John Lynch, John McKeone, John Michael Sears, John O'Malley, John Scarsborough, John Short, John Sudgen, John Tatum, John Terpstra, John Vale, John Wheway, John Whitehouse, John Younger, Jonathan Attrill, Jonathan Jones, Jonathan Young, Joolz Denby, Joseph Allen, Joseph Desmond, Joseph Estevez, Josephine Dickinson, Josephine Greenland, Josephine von Zitzewitz, Judith Drazin, Judith Drazin, Judith Wilkinson, Julia Ciesielska, Julia Davis, Julia Deakin, Julian Cason, Julian Matthews, Julian Stannard, Juliana Mensah, Julie Baber, Julie Egdell, Julie Irigaray, Julie Kafka, Julie Lumsden, Julie Sheridan, Julie Venner, June Wentland, Justin Lloyde, K.V.Skene, Karen Dennison, Karen Little, Karen Simecek, Karl Egerton, Karl Riordan, Kat Couch, Kate Marshall-Flaherty, Kate Rhodes, Kate Scott, Kate Stevens, Kate Symons, Katherine Gallagher, Katherine Lawrence, Kathleen McPhilemy, Kathleen Strafford, Kathrin Schmidt, Kathryn Daszkiewicz, Kathryn Haworth, Kathryn Moores, Kathy Gee, Katie Campbell, Keith Armstrong, Keith Willson, Kelley J White, Kemal Houghton, Ken Champion, Ken Gambles, Kenneth Durham Smith, Kenneth Steven, Kerry Andrew, Kevan Youde, Kevin Armor Harris, Kevin Watson, Khadija Rouf, Kieran Egan, Kieran Furey, Kim Moore, Kit Habianic, Knotbrook Taylor, Konye Obaji Ori, Krishan Coupland, Kristy Kerruish, L Kiew, Lance Nizami, Laura Mason, Laura Potts, Laura Strickland, Lauren K. Nixon, Laurence Bainbridge, Laurie Kruk, Lawrence Bradby, Lawrence Mathias, Lesley Quayle, Linda Dawe, Linda Lee Welch, Linda Marshall), Linda Rose Parkes, Lisa Falshaw, Lisa Parry, Liz McPherson, Liz Proctor, Lizzie Holden, Lotte Kramer, Louise Ayre, Louise Warren, Louise Wilford, Lucie McKee, Lucy Brennan, Lucy Heuschen, Luis Benitez, Luke Burford, Lydia Popowich, Lynda Plater, Lynn Valentine, Maggie Davison, Maggie Mackay, Maggie Mealy, Maggie Nicholls, Maitreyabandhu, Malcolm Carson, Malcolm Povey, Malcolm Venn, Mandy Coe, Mandy Haggith, Marc Swan, Marek Urbanowicz, Marg Roberts, Margaret Poynor-Clark, Margaret Speck, Maria Castro Dominguez, Maria Stephenson, Marian Homans Berges, Marie Papier, Marilyn Donovan, Marilyn Francis, Mario Petrucci, Mario Susko, Marion Ashton, Marion Hobday, Marion Oxley, Marius Grose, Mark Anthony Kaye, Mark Arvid White, Mark Carew, Mark Carson, Mark Connors, Mark Czanik, Mark Czanik, Mark Farrell, Mark Goodwin, Mark Jarman, Mark Patrick Lynch, Mark Pearce, Mark Pirie, Mark Wasserman, Mark Wilmot, Marlene Hetschko, Martha Glaser, Martin Malone, Martin Matthews, Martin Reed, Martin Stannard, Martyn Crucefix, Mary Anne Smith Sellen, Mary Corkery, Mary Earnshaw, Mary Michaels, Mary Warner, Marylou Grimberg, Mat Riches, Mathilda Oosthuizen, Matt Black, Matt Simpson, Matthew Clegg, Matthew Friday, Matthew Smith, Matthew Twigg, Matthias Claudius, Maureen Hynes, Max Watt, Megan Owen, Melissa Lee, Menno Wigman, Meredith Andrea, Merryn Williams, Mia Lofthouse, Michael Bartholomew-Biggs, Michael Blackburn, Michael Church, Michael Curtis, Michael Henry, Michael Lamb, Michael McGill, Michael Newman, Michael Parr, Michael Penny, Michael Prior, Michael Spring, Michael Swan, Michael Thomas, Michael Wyndham, Michelle Scally, Mick Jenkinson, Mike Alderson, Mike Barlow, Mike Farren, Mike Hoy, Mike Jenkins, Mike McNamara, Mike O'Brien, Miles Larmour, Miles Salter, Milner Place, Mimi Khalvati, Mims Sully, Miranda Day, Miriam Patrick, Miriam Sulhunt, Moez Surani, Moira Garland, Myra Schneider, Nancy Ford Duggan, Natalie Fry, Natalie Fry, Natalie Scott, Nathan Evans, Nathan Fidler, Neil Beardmore, Neil Campbell, Neil Elder, Neil Rathmell, Neil Windsor, Neile Graham, Nell Farell, Ness Al-Shaikly, Neville Judson, Niall McGrath, Niall Spooner-Harvey, Nicholas Bielby, Nicholas Lee, Nicholas McGaughey, Nick Allen, Nick Armitage, Nick Boreham, Nick Cooke, Nick Pearson, Nick Toczek, Nicola Bray, Nicola Daly, Nicolas Spicer, Niels Hammer, Nigel Barton, Nigel Ferrier Collins, Nigel Forde, Nigel Jarrett, Nigel Pickard, Nigel Prentice, Nigel Walker, Nii Ayikwei Parkes, Nina Boyd, Noel King, Noel Williams, Nora Nadjarian, Norah Hanson, Norbert Hirschhorn, Norman Harrington, Norman Jackson, Nuala Ni Chonchuir, Oana Avasilichioaei, Oda Dellagi, Odilia Gartner, Oleg Okhapkin, Orlanda Marsden, Owen Gallagher, Owen O'Sullivan, Oz Hardwick, P.F. Brownsey, P.K. Page, Pam Thompson, Pamela Coren, Pamela Lewis, Pamela Scobie, Pamela Scott, Pat Borthwick, Pat Earnshaw, Pat Simmons, Patricia Cleveland-Peck, Patricia Leighton, Patrick Druggan, Patrick Friesen, Patrick Lodge, Patrick Wright, Patrick Yarker, Paul Brownsey, Paul Connolly, Paul Durrant, Paul Garvey, Paul Groves, Paul Mein, Paul Mills, Paul Mullen, Paul Saville, Paul Surman, Paul Sutherland, Paul Vaughan, Paula Jennings, Pauline Kirk, Penelope Weiss, Penny Blackburn, Penny Feeny, Penny Frances, Penny Sharman, Penny Wheatley, Pete Morgan, Peter Adams, Peter Burrows, Peter Dale, Peter Datyner, Peter Day, Peter Farrell, Peter Gilmour, Peter J King, Peter King, Peter Knaggs, Peter Lewin, Phil Connolly, Phil Knight, Phil Knight., Phil Vernon, Phil Walsh, Philip Beverley, Philip Burton, Philip Dunkerley, Philip Dunn, Philip Walsh, Philippa East, PJ Quinn, PJ Stephenson, Poppy Bristow, R.G. Jodah, R.J. Powell, Rachel Bower, Rachel Kerr, Rand Allan Kennedy, Rani Drew, Ray Malone, Rebecca Buchanan, Rebecca West, Rebecca Wood, Rene and David Gill, Rennie Parker, Reza Ghahremanzadeh, Rhys Harrison, Richard Berry, Richard Biddle, Richard Cave, Richard George, Richard Kitchen, Richard Lister, Richard Livermore, River Wolton, Rob Hindle, Rob Miles, Rob Peel, Robert Etty, Robert Ford, Robert Karl Harding, Robert Lima, Robert Nightingale, Robert Nisbet, Robert O'Connor, Robert Powell, Robert Rothman, Robin Fine and Oz Hardwick, Robin Ford, Robin Lindsay Wilson, Robin Maunsel, Robin Renwick, Robin Vaughan-Williams, Roddy Williams, Rodie Sudbery, Roger Caldwell, Roger Hare, Roger Harvey, Roger Perrin, Roger Turner, Roman Mikheenkov, Ron Wilson, Ronan Corrigan, Rory MacCallum, Rory Waterman, Rosalie Garland, Rosamund Davies, Rose Drew, Rose Flint, Rosemary Collins, Rosemary Hector, Rosemary Mitchell-Schuitevoerder, Rosemary Norman, Rosie Garner, Ross Kightly, Roy Duffield, Roy Marshall, Roy Sutirtha, Roz Goddard, Rupert M Loyell, Russell Thornton, Ruth Aylett, Ruth Beckett, Ruth Hardy, Ruth Kelsey, Ruth O'Callaghan, Ruth Sharman, Ryan Bowd, S. P. Hannaway, Sally Festing, Sally Long, Sally Read, Sally Spedding, Sam Duda, Sam Gardiner, Sam Garvan, Sam Kemp, Sam Smith, Sam Smith, Sandra Galton, Sandra Noel, Sarah Hills, Sarah L Dixon, Sarah

Wallis, Sarah Williams, Sarah Wimbush, Scott Butterworth, Scott Elder, Sean Body, Sean Burn, Sean Howard, Sebastian Barker, Selma Meerbaum-Eisinger, Seth Crook, Sextus Porpertius, Shanta Acharya, Sharon Overend, Sharp Weather, Sheema Kalbasi, Sheila Aldous, Sheila Endersby, Sheila Jacob, Sheri Young, Shijini Singh, Shirley Golden, Simon Beech, Simon Cockle, Simon Currie, Simon Fletcher, Simon Fletcher, Simon French, Simon Haines, Simon Howells, Simon Robson, Simon Tindale, Siobhan Harvey, Sky Martin, S M Steele , Sophie Reynolds, Stanley M. Noah, Stanley Noah, Stephanie Conybeare, Stephanie Powell, Stephen Capus, Stephen Devereux, Stephen Loveless, Stephen Wade, Stepten Saul, Steve Allen, Steve Beadle, Steve Dalzell, Steve Garrett, Steve Harrison, Steve Komarnyckyj, Steve Smith, Steve Sneyd, Steven Blyth, Steven Lightfoot, Steven Maxwell, Steven Sivell, Steven Waling, Stewart Lowe, Stuart Handysides, Stuart Pickford, Stuart Sinclair, Sue Butler, Sue Guiney, Sue Johns, Sue Moules, Sue Spiers, Sue Watling, Sue Wood, Susan Darlington, Susan Ioannou , Susan Mary Wade, Susan Sciama, Susan Wallace, Susan Wicks, Susana Morvan, Susanna Harding, Susie Williamson, Suzannah Evans, Suzanne Batty, T.Anders Carson, T.F. Griffin, Taliesin Gore, Tammi Cottingham, Tanvir Ratul, Tanya Parker Nightingale, Tariq Latif, Teddy Goldstein, Terence Dooley, Teresa Forrest, Terry Dammery, Terry Griffiths, Terry Jones, Terry Kay, Terry Sherwood, Tess Jolly, Tess Nile, Tessa Harmse, Thelma Laycock, Thomas Clark, Thomas Dixon, Thomas Morgan, Tim Dwyer, Tim Love, Tim Phillips, Timothy Houghton, Toby Martinez de las Rivas, Tom Bryan, Tom Dixon, Tom Heaton, Tom Sharp, Tom Vaughan, Tom Weir, Tom Wigan, Tom Yates, Tonnie Richmond, Tony Cosier , Tony Flynn, Tony Hendry, Tony Lucas, Tony McCabe, Tony Roberts, Tracey Iceton, Tracy Dawson, Tyler Keevil , Val Horner, Valerie McLeod, Verity Baldry, Victor Tapner, Victoria Dowd, Victoria Gatehouse, Vincent Wood, Vyacheslav Kovalsky, W.H.Petty, Wendy Cope, Wendy French, Wendy Klein, Wendy Pratt, Wilf Deckne, Will Kemp, William Alderson, William Alderson, William Bedford, William Coniston, William Oxley, William Park, William Spencer, Yvonne Carter, Yvonne Hendrie, Zarina Yousuf-Bonass, Zoe Brooks,

Other anthologies and collections available from Stairwell Books

Goldfish	Jonathan Aylett
Strike	Sarah Wimbush
Marginalia	Doreen Hinchliffe
The Estuary and the Sea	Jennifer Keevill
In | Between	Angela Arnold
Quiet Flows the Hull	Clint Wastling
Lunch on a Green Ledge	Stella Davis
there is an england	Harry Gallagher
Iconic Tattoo	Richard Harries
Fatherhood	CS Fuqua
Herdsmenization	Ngozi Olivia Osuoha
On the Other Side of the Beach, Light	Daniel Skyle
Words from a Distance	Ed. Amina Alyal, Judi Sissons
Fractured	Shannon O'Neill
Unknown	Anna Rose James, Elizabeth Chadwick Pywell
When We Wake We Think We're Whalers from Eden	Bob Beagrie
Awakening	Richard Harries
Starspin	Graehame Barrasford Young
A Stray Dog, Following	Greg Quiery
Blue Saxophone	Rosemary Palmeira
Steel Tipped Snowflakes 1	Izzy Rhiannon Jones, Becca Miles, Laura Voivodeship
Where the Hares Are	John Gilham
The Glass King	Gary Allen
A Thing of Beauty Is a Joy Forever	Don Walls
Gooseberries	Val Horner
Poetry for the Newly Single 40 Something	Maria Stephenson
Northern Lights	Harry Gallagher
Nothing Is Meant to be Broken	Mark Connors
Heading for the Hills	Gillian Byrom-Smith
More Exhibitionism	Ed. Glen Taylor
The Beggars of York	Don Walls
Lodestone	Hannah Stone
Unsettled Accounts	Tony Lucas
Learning to Breathe	John Gilham
Throwing Mother in the Skip	William Thirsk-Gaskill
New Crops from Old Fields	Ed. Oz Hardwick
The Ordinariness of Parrots	Amina Alyal
Somewhere Else	Don Walls

For further information please contact rose@stairwellbooks.com

www.stairwellbooks.co.uk
@stairwellbooks